# THE GREAT HISPANIC HERITAGE

# Oscar De La Hoya

# THE GREAT HISPANIC HERITAGE

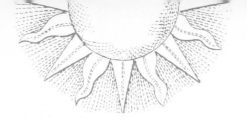

# THE GREAT HISPANIC HERITAGE

# Oscar De La Hoya

Susan Muaddi Darraj and Rob Maaddi

CHELSEA HOUSE
PUBLISHERS
An imprint of Infobase Publishing

**Oscar De La Hoya**

Copyright © 2008 by Infobase Publishing

Chelsea House
An imprint of Infobase Publishing
132 West 31st Street
New York NY 10001

**Library of Congress Cataloging-in-Publication Data**

Darraj, Susan Muaddi.
  Oscar De La Hoya / Susan Muaddi Darraj and Rob Maaddi.
      p. cm. — (The great Hispanic heritage)
  Includes bibliographical references and index.
  ISBN 978-0-7910-9692-5 (hardcover)
  1. De La Hoya, Oscar, 1973—Juvenile literature. 2. Boxers (Sports)—United
States—Biography—Juvenile literature. I. Maaddi, Rob. II. Title. III. Series.
  GV1132.D37D37 2008
  796.83092—dc22        2007032007

Text design by Takeshi Takahashi
Cover design by Keith Trego and Jooyoung An

Printed in the United States of America

Bang EJB 10 9 8 7 6 5 4 3 2 1

This book is printed on acid-free paper.

All links and Web addresses were checked and verified to be correct at the time of publication. Because of the dynamic nature of the Web, some addresses and links may have changed since publication and may no longer be valid.

# Contents

# Winning the Gold

**Cecilia De La Hoya was dying of cancer. She had been dying** for some time. When Cecilia was first diagnosed with breast cancer, only her husband, Joel Sr., knew it. She had tried to protect her children from the terrible truth while she underwent various treatments, including chemotherapy and radiation. She especially did not want her second son, Oscar, to know about her condition.

For 11 years, since he was six years old, Oscar had been dedicated to one goal: becoming a professional boxer. The idea, however, had not been his. It was that of his father, Joel De La Hoya Sr., a former amateur boxer himself. Since the first time he had stepped into the ring, Oscar had been told that he had to win, no matter what. Joel Sr. applied the pressure. Oscar's mom, Cecilia, helped him to release it.

Cecilia was a seamstress, who worked long hours to help support her family of three children: Joel Jr., Oscar, and

Oscar De La Hoya is considered one of the all-time boxing champions. He has won six world titles in six different weight classes and an Olympic gold medal. As an amateur boxer, De La Hoya posted an amazing 223-5 record with 163 knockouts.

Cecilia, the baby of the family whom everyone called "Ceci." Cecilia, like her husband, wanted to see her son become a boxing champion, but she also wanted him to be happy. By all accounts, she was one of the few people to whom young Oscar could talk openly about his feelings, his emotions, and his private thoughts. A former singer, Cecilia often indulged her son by singing to him and was thrilled when he would join her.

The family lived in East Los Angeles, California. It was a rough neighborhood, and life there was difficult. The area was plagued with crime and drugs, and for many young men, the only route to getting out and "making it big" was to succeed in the boxing ring. Few amateur boxers, however, showed the promise that Oscar demonstrated. Everyone in the family, including aunts, uncles, and cousins, knew that Oscar's fists could one day lift them all out of the ghetto.

In order not to distract Oscar from his training, Cecilia kept the truth largely to herself. In fact, in August 1990, she skipped a week of radiation treatments just to attend Oscar's fight at the Goodwill Games, where he was the youngest fighter to ever compete in the event. Proudly, she watched her son as he defeated his opponent and won the gold medal. Medically, however, things were growing worse for her. She knew it was time to tell him of her serious illness.

## A PROMISE

Tim Kawakami, author of the Oscar De La Hoya biography, *Golden Boy: The Fame, Money and Mystery of Oscar De La Hoya*, writes of their mother's illness, "The De La Hoya boys were in denial."[1] Both Joel Jr. and Oscar were stunned by the news of their mother's condition, but they could not understand or accept how serious their beloved mother's illness really was. Only their sister, Ceci, who spent more time with their mother, could see the inevitable.

Perhaps that was because mother Cecilia downplayed the situation to her sons, saying, "Don't worry about me. I'll be

As a young boy, De La Hoya never thought about becoming a fighter. He enjoyed playing baseball in the park and skateboarding with his friends near his house. His older brother, Joel Jr., claimed that Oscar was never violent, saying, "Oscar hated physical confrontations. He never had a street fight."

okay. Don't worry."[2] Yet, Oscar steadily became more aware of what was happening, especially when he saw that the therapy made her hair fall out.

The situation put pressure on Joel Sr. as well, for he was working full-time in addition to managing his son's boxing career. Coming up with money for Cecilia's cancer treatments proved to be a tremendous challenge, and he often sought out help from some of the scouts and managers who had their eyes on Oscar. Joel Sr. knew that his son would be a hot commodity one day, so he used the only card he could play, promising managers that Oscar would sign with them once he turned professional. In return, he received money, which he used to pay his wife's mounting hospital bills.

In the end, though, nothing could help Cecilia. In October 1990, her condition became even worse. Oscar recalls one of the last conversations he had with her, when she was still lucid and aware of her surroundings. "She told me she was very confident after watching me win the Goodwill Games. . . . She told me, 'I want you to win the gold medal.'"[3]

Cecilia was referring to the Olympic Games, which would be held in Barcelona, Spain, in 1992. Everyone's hopes were pinned on Oscar to win the gold medal, an achievement that would launch his career into professional boxing. Cecilia, however, knew she would not be there to see him win. On October 29, 1990, she died. She was only 38 years old. Oscar was not with her when she passed away. Instead, he showed up at the hospital later for a visit, only to be told the devastating news.

Oscar kept his emotions inside until her funeral. He was the only member of the family to cry at his mother's burial, and he did that "loudly and stirringly. He mourned her hard. For the first time anyone could remember, the pensive little boy was letting the world see how he felt, exposing himself as he broke into pieces. For his mother."[4]

For a while after her death, Oscar toyed with the idea of quitting boxing. He was going through a phase where he questioned the importance and the relevance of everything in his life. Yet, he remembered the promise he had made to his mother that he would bring back the gold medal from Barcelona. Then, when he came home, he would place it at her gravestone and dedicate it to her.

# Growing Up
# in the Barrio

When you enter the east side of Los Angeles, a sign in Spanish that reads *Bienvenidos*, or "Welcome," greets you. The neighborhood, known as "East L.A.," includes approximately 125,000 people. It is predominantly Spanish-speaking, with a high number of immigrants from Mexico and other Latin-American countries. Some have lived in East L.A. for generations, while some have recently arrived from other countries.

Southern California is a diverse community in general, but East Los Angeles is a special case. The Latin-American community here is the largest in the United States, and the people of the neighborhood are quite proud of their heritage and culture. Yet, the community is also plagued with problems, most of which are related to poverty and gang violence. The area is economically depressed, with the per capita, or

Gang violence is a major problem in Los Angeles, California. Here, Los Angeles Police Department officers surround a man suspected of a crime. According to police accounts, about 250 Latino gangs operate in the Los Angeles area.

per person, income under $10,000 per year. The average household income is slightly over $30,000 per year. Roughly one third of the population lives below the federal government's poverty line. Furthermore, high school dropout rates are some of the highest in the country, and unemployment is very high.

In this poor economic climate, gangs rule some of the streets in East L.A. The entire city of Los Angeles is home to approximately 500 separate gangs. They are usually highly organized and have access to guns and other weapons. The gangs often fund themselves through the sales of illegal drugs. According to the Los Angeles Police Department, Latino gangs are the most numerous, with over 22,000 members in almost 250 gangs. Many of these gangs operate within the East Los Angeles section of the city.

Many of the gangs take part in turf wars, going into one another's claimed territories to commit robberies and other crimes. The Maravilla gangs are some of the oldest gangs in the region and originated in East L.A., which was originally known as *Maravilla,* or "marvelous." Another gang is the Mexican Mafia, which has a history dating back to the 1950s. The homicide rates associated with gang violence are startling. Almost half of the homicides in the city in 2005, for example, were related to gang activity. In other words, to grow up in East L.A., a person needs to know how to defend himself. That means knowing how to fight.

Perhaps that is the reason why boxing is one of the premier sports that is glorified in East L.A. In this neighborhood where respect is based on being tough, knowing how to use your hands to take down an opponent is a vital skill to possess. In his biography of Oscar De La Hoya, Kawakami claims that "boxing was not art, it was survival. Winning was about persevering, and about ferociousness. . . ."[5]

Yet, as a young boy, Oscar De La Hoya hardly seemed that he would grow up to be East L.A.'s most celebrated boxing champion. In fact, his father pushed his youngest son to get involved in boxing not because he thought he would be a great fighter. Instead, "he sent him for self-defense."[6]

## THE DE LA HOYA BOXING HERITAGE

Boxing is a tradition in the De La Hoya family. Oscar was fated to be involved in the sport in some way, although nobody could have predicted the level of his future achievements. Oscar's grandfather, Vincente De La Hoya, had fought in the featherweight class (under 126 pounds, or 57kg) in his

Oscar De La Hoya's grandfather, Vincente, came from Durango, Mexico. The area was a favorite location for making films, especially cowboy Westerns. Here, Bob Dylan appears in the 1973 film, *Pat Garrett & Billy the Kid*. Vincente De La Hoya left Mexico for California in 1956.

hometown of Durango, located in the northwest region of Mexico. Durango was actually a popular place for American filmmakers, who shot many Westerns along its scenic streets and featured its landscapes in movies. In 1956, Vincente De La Hoya emigrated to the United States, taking most of his large family with him. (He had been married twice and he had 16 children.) Vincente settled in Southern California, which is where most Mexican émigrés landed and was joined in 1957 by his son Joel, also an amateur boxer.

Joel fought in the lightweight division, or 130 to 135 pounds (59kg to 61kg). He had made a name for himself fighting in Durango, and he hoped to build a boxing career in the United States. The burden of immigration, however, proved to be harsh, and it became necessary to support the family. Joel had to get a job as soon as possible. He attempted to fight and work out in the evenings after work, but his schedule was too rigorous, and he eventually accepted the fact that he had to abandon his boxing ambitions.

In 1969, Joel Sr. met Cecilia Gonzalez. She was 17 years old and working as a seamstress. She also was known locally for her lovely singing voice, and she sang occasionally for extra money, both back home in Mexico as a child and as a newly arrived immigrant in the United States. Some sources state that she had a professional singing career in Mexico, although it is hard to verify that information. (In some interviews, Oscar De La Hoya refers to his mother as having been a "professional" singer.) Joel was 27 years old, 10 years older than Cecilia, but despite the age difference, he fell deeply in love with her. He pursued her eagerly and was persistent, and his efforts paid off. Joel and Cecilia married a short while later, then had three children. Their first child was named Joel Jr., after his father. Oscar was born on February 4, 1973, and his sister, Cecilia, named for her mother, came almost a decade later.

Joel Sr. worked as a shipping clerk, and Cecilia continued doing seamstress work as much as possible. They lived in a small house on South McDonnell Avenue in the southern part of their Latin-American neighborhood, surrounded by other family members. The De La Hoyas counted many among their numbers, and while money was always an issue,

Oscar claimed that "we never felt poor. . . . We always felt like we had everything."[7]

Oscar's grandfather, Vincente, owned a restaurant, Virginia's Place, and it became a hangout for the De La Hoya family. Joel Sr. and Cecilia's children always had good clothing and the essentials, but there were times when Oscar felt the strain that poverty had placed on his family. The family, like many in their neighborhood, depended on food stamps, and Cecilia often sent the children to the corner store to buy groceries with the stamps. For Oscar, this often proved to be embarrassing, even humiliating.

Whenever his mother asked him to go to the store, he would protest, and even cry, to avoid going. Once when his mother forced him to go, he found several other customers in the store. He waited for almost an hour in the store until all the customers had paid and left before taking his purchases to the counter. When the clerk asked him what had taken him so long to make his purchase, he admitted that he did not want anyone to see him paying with food stamps, despite the fact that many others in the neighborhood also relied on them to make necessary grocery purchases.

His parents often became frustrated with Oscar, who proved to have a very sensitive and emotional side to him. In many ways, he was different than his older brother, Joel Jr., who was a tough, assertive person, even as a child. Joel Jr. had a lot of athletic prowess and ability, and naturally his father assumed that he would follow in his footsteps and pursue boxing. For Joel Sr., giving up boxing had been a difficult thing to do, and, more than anything, he wanted one of his sons to have the boxing career he had to abandon. Joel Jr., however, preferred baseball to boxing and soon made it clear to his father that boxing was not in his future. The decision caused a great rift between father and son. Joel Sr. then turned to his second son, the more unlikely boxing prospect: the scrawny, skinny, and sensitive Oscar.

## THE EASTSIDE BOXING CLUB

Oscar De La Hoya was six years old when he was first thrust into the boxing ring by his zealous, ambitious father. Despite his small size and sensitive nature, before long, he soon surprised even his greatest skeptics. Oscar had long been protected from the pressure to box because Joel Sr. had focused on his older son to follow in his footsteps. That left Oscar relatively free to skateboard and do other things he enjoyed. Eventually, however, he realized he would have to step inside the ring and at least attempt to live up to his father's dreams.

Yet, he had not had a good experience with boxing to this point. A short time before he stepped into the ring, his brother

## THE HISPANIC HERITAGE IN LOS ANGELES

The Hispanic roots of Los Angeles are deeply embedded in the city's history. Los Angeles, America's second most populous city, was originally part of Mexico. After the Mexican-American War (1846–1848) ended, the territory was granted to the United States by Mexico in a treaty.

Many people call Los Angeles the capital of Mexamerica, a reference to the growing Latino, especially Mexican-American, presence in the United States. Latinos currently form the most numerous ethnic minority in the United States, and much of the population is located in areas close to the Mexican border, such as Southern California. Forty-eight percent of the population of Los Angeles County is Latin American.

Los Angeles is the home of the movie and music industry in the United States, much of which has been influenced and shaped by the city's Hispanic heritage. Furthermore, many Latin-American writers and artists hail from Los Angeles, which is also known as the City of Angels. The Los Angeles Latino International Film Festival (LALIFF) and the Los Angeles Latino Book & Family Festival are two examples of the Latino roots of the city.

set up a boxing bout between Oscar and one of their younger cousins. Oscar recalled, "[He] put a pair [of gloves] on me and the other pair on one of my cousins. Then he yelled 'Time!' Immediately, I covered my cheeks with the gloves. The next thing I knew—wham—the first punch is a left jab that goes between my gloves and lands smack on my nose!"[8] As he tells it, Oscar ran home crying.

Located six blocks from Oscar's home on South McDonnell Avenue, the Eastside Boxing Club was managed by Joe Minjarez, who had seen many great fighters come and go. Minjarez was probably the first skeptic, the first to shake his head and wonder what Joel De La Hoya Sr. was thinking when he brought in his skinny son to the club. Not only was the child nonconfrontational (he was known in the neighborhood as a kid who ran away from fights), but he also had a high, soft voice that he had inherited from his mother, the singer, and a face that people described as delicate, with fine features. Furthermore, Oscar was left-handed. Minjarez was training four other young boxers, all right-handed, and he did not want to throw a lefty into the group.

Minjarez, however, soon realized that Oscar's left hand could land a devastating blow to an opponent in the ring. The problem was that Oscar could only awkwardly lead with his right hand. During training one day, Minjarez had Oscar try something new, later recalling, "I turned him around, and he caught on *like that.*"[9] By leading with his stronger left hand, Oscar was able to knock his opponents off balance. Immediately, Oscar began to dominate his sparring partners, pounding the other boxers with his powerful left hand, now being used as a jab or hook. In addition to his devastating power, Oscar also demonstrated a natural grace in the ring. He seemingly danced around his opponents in the ring and then landed his blows with deadly accuracy.

Oscar fought his first fight when he was seven years old against a slightly more experienced youngster in his weight division. Oscar won the fight easily, in the third round, then ran back to his father and said the words that Joel Sr. thought he would never hear from his younger son: "Poppy, I like it!"[10] Oscar liked it even more when he realized that for every fight he won, his father, aunts, and uncles would reward him with fifty cents or a dollar. As a child, he looked at boxing as a job or as a way to earn extra spending money. Little did he know that he would eventually be earning millions of dollars.

# 3

# The Development of a Champion

As Oscar De La Hoya steadily won fight after fight and knocked down one sparring partner after another, he developed a reputation as a fierce fighter. Outside of the ring, he seemed like a small, skinny kid, but once he stepped inside and faced his challenger, he unleashed a torrent of power and fury in his punches. Joe Minjarez, the manager of the Eastside Boxing Club, claims that he even had problems finding sparring partners for Oscar because "nobody wanted to fight him."[11]

Joel Sr. realized the raw talent that his son possessed. It was mostly Oscar's terrifyingly powerful left hand but also his style in the ring and his killer instinct that contributed to the steady building of a winning record. Although Oscar was only a child, his father recognized the makings of a champion. He began putting pressure on Oscar, who, unlike his older brother, did not complain. When he was told to get up and get to the gym to work out and practice, he did as he was told, despite the rigorous schedule.

When he was eight years old, he was entered in the Freewill Games, where he placed first, making him the youngest contender ever to do so. By that point, people in the East L.A. barrio started to take notice of the change in Oscar. They no longer regarded him as a scrawny kid who skateboarded along the streets and cried at fights. Instead, in a Latin-American neighborhood where boxing had paved the way for famous fighters, people started to consider the possibility that Oscar would be a future champion.

Even before he was 14 years old, Oscar had fought in over 100 bouts, winning all but two of them. At the age of 15, he fought in a Golden Gloves Tournament, one of his first major fights. Under the supervision of his father and Joe Minjarez, Oscar had taken part in many other tournaments before. Each time, he gave a stellar performance. At the Golden Gloves, his opponent was Manuel Nava, who also had an excellent reputation in the ring. Joel Sr. and Minjarez wondered how Oscar would fare against this rival, but Oscar surprised them by knocking Nava down three times and winning the fight. He also knocked out and defeated another amateur fighter who was nine years older than himself and more experienced.

Oscar's fierceness in the ring probably had its origin in his frustrations. Despite the fact that his father was pleased with him and excited about Oscar's possible future boxing career, Oscar never had a positive relationship with Joel Sr. Though he was not afraid of his father, he resented some of the pressure put on him to win. As he grew older, he also started to somewhat resent the rigorous training schedule imposed on him. He wanted more free time to spend with his friends, but Joel Sr. would not stand for it. He wanted Oscar's attention to be focused almost exclusively on boxing, day and night.

If Oscar wanted to relax after school one day and lounge on the sofa, rather than attend his rigorous training session, Joel Sr. would become enraged. If Oscar wanted to stay up late and hang out with his friends, his father would angrily remind him that he had to wake up early for his training session. The training sessions he attended consisted of running, sparring, weight lifting, and other strenuous activities that required absolute dedication and commitment; traits that not every teenage boy possesses.

When his father would push him and fight with him about these issues, Oscar would become furious and even consider dropping boxing, as his older brother had done. The pressure was too high at some points to make him want to stick with it. He even missed his senior prom, an occasion all high school kids look forward to, because he was out of town participating in a tournament in North Carolina.

From Joel Sr.'s point, however, he recognized that his son had a unique talent, and he did not want him to squander his time on social activities. Joel Sr. believed that the stakes were too high, and, if Oscar could be more committed, it would pay off for his young son in the end. During these rough times, Cecilia De La Hoya became the peacemaker in the family. Oscar could always talk to her and explain his feelings, and she listened patiently, helping him to calm down and try to understand his father. Furthermore, Oscar always respected his father, even though he felt like venting his anger. De La Hoya later recalled, "Man, it's like inside the ring is where I used to unleash all my frustrations. If I was mad at my father that day or anything, I used to go crazy. I used to be crazy inside the ring."[12]

## EYES ON THE OLYMPICS

Joel Sr. and Oscar both set their sights on the Olympics. Everyone knew that a superb performance in the Olympic Games was the perfect way to launch a professional boxing career. That would, in turn, lead to the possibility of earning big money in the ring.

The rules of amateur boxing in the United States include the important fact that the winner is not rewarded with a cash purse, or prize money. For the De La Hoyas, who were living off Joel Sr.'s small salary, it was important to put Oscar in a position where he could eventually earn big dollars. In fact, the entire family had begun to view Oscar as its future breadwinner. Oscar later recalled, "When I was winning tournaments, growing up, fourteen or fifteen, everybody would put all the attention to me . . . uncles and aunts and our parents."[13]

Oscar's amateur record was stellar, and he already earned a number of titles. In 1988, at age 15, he won the U.S. Junior

## THE SPORT OF BOXING

Boxing has also been known as prizefighting, possibly because the winner traditionally receives a purse, or monetary reward. Boxing is a combat sport, in which two opponents in the same weight division fight hand-to-hand in a series of rounds, each lasting one to three minutes. The way to win is to knock out one's opponent. If both fighters are still standing at the end of the bout, a panel of judges determines the winner, using a point system based on the fighters' performance in each round.

The origins of boxing can probably be traced back to about 3,000 B.C., to the ancient Berbers and Egyptians of northern Africa. Later, it was one of the events in the original Olympics in Greece, in which fighters wore leather straps wound around their hands for protection. In 1743, Englishman Jack Broughton, a boxing champion, introduced the first official rules of the sport, including a rule in which fighters could not strike at an opponent who was down on the ground. The rules were drawn up in an effort to prevent deaths in the ring, which happened because of the former no-holds-barred policy. Later, more specific rules

Olympic 119-pound (54 kg) title. The next year, he won the national Golden Gloves. In 1990, at 125 pounds (57 kg), De La Hoya then won the U.S. amateur title. That same year, the young boxer captured the gold medal in the Goodwill Games in Seattle. At every fight, whenever he won, people could not help but notice the handsome, young man with the baby face who was a fierce tiger in the ring. Everywhere he went, people seemed to instinctively know he would be a future champion.

By this time, Oscar was attending Garfield High School, one of the largest in East L.A. It was the same school at which math professor Jaime Escalante (whose education ambitions and teaching successes were immortalized in the film *Stand and Deliver*) won national recognition for teaching calculus.

were put into effect, such as the banning of head butting, biting, and other offenses.

The world of boxing operates on both amateur and professional levels. Amateur boxing can be found at the collegiate level, at the Olympic Games, at the Commonwealth Games, and in countless venues, ranging in scope from local to international events. Amateur boxers wear protective headgear and gloves with a white strip across the knuckles that help judges determine the effectiveness of the boxer's punches. Amateur fights are short in duration. Professional bouts usually range from 10 to 12 rounds, although shorter fights do occur. Professional boxers do not wear any protective headgear. The most common boxing punches include:

*Jab* A quick, straight punch thrown with the lead hand

*Hook* A semicircular punch thrown with the lead hand to the side of the opponent's head.

*Cross* A powerful straight punch thrown with the rear hand

*Uppercut* A vertical, rising punch thrown with the rear hand

De La Hoya was too busy with building his boxing career, however, to focus much on school. In fact, he was often out of class, on the road, traveling to different tournaments. When he did attend class, he was usually exhausted from early morning workouts and training sessions.

Oscar's principal at Garfield High, Maria Elena Tostado, fondly remembered him, saying, "He was just so single-minded, preparing for his fights. He knew what he wanted and he wanted it from day one. I never would've picked him out as a fighter. When I first met him, someone told me he was going to the Olympics, and I thought it was a joke. He was the most quiet, unassuming young man you'd ever want to meet. Super nice. Super humble."[14]

Many people agreed that Oscar De La Hoya was a polite young man who did not cause trouble. Yet, getting into the ring with him, as many opponents had already discovered, was a different story. In the ring, the hard-hitting Oscar's ferocious, competitive side emerged.

## WINNING THE GOLD

As he prepared to go to the 1992 Olympics in Barcelona, Oscar was filled with confidence. His amateur record was amazing, and he had racked up a series of wins by knockouts. He had every right to be sure of himself. On an Olympic poster, he wrote, "92 Champ." This was, as *Golden Boy* author Kawakami says, "a cocky promise, from a child to himself."[15] De La Hoya himself claimed, "I knew I was going to do something, even then. That was my goal, my dream."[16]

His preparations for Barcelona, however, were brought to a jarring halt when his mother, Cecilia, died of breast cancer. Oscar was devastated and considered dropping out from boxing altogether. He felt that he had no ambition left to be competitive. Yet, he recalled his mother's words to him, to win the gold at the Olympics, and he remembered his promise to her that he would do it. He pushed on with his goals, training harder than ever. He dedicated every win to his mother, remembering that she was his inspiration. In fact, every time he won a fight, he fell to his knees and blew a kiss upward, to his mother in heaven. "It's just a way of saying, 'For you,'" he explained when asked about it.[17] It was a way for him to remind himself that it was his mother who had re-energized his dedication to boxing.

At the Olympics, Oscar had to win five fights, each three rounds, to win the gold medal. He was anxious and nervous upon landing in Barcelona, and he wanted nothing more than to get in the ring and get on with it. Before the tournament, De La Hoya remarked, "There's a lot of pressure when you're favored to win the gold. Some guys are coming into this with nothing to lose. They're just here for respect. But the pressure is on me. I'm expected to win. That pushes me harder in training. I'm only nineteen, though, and it's tough sometimes. I've been thinking about winning a gold medal for six years. I put everything on hold for this."[18]

Indeed, Oscar had put a lot on hold for this single event. He had spent most of his youth in the boxing ring—endlessly sparring, training, and fighting—rather than living the normal life of a teenaged boy. Now he had to prove to himself—and his father—that it had all been worth it.

De La Hoya fought in the 132-pound (60 kg) weight division. His first fight was against Adilson Silva, a Brazilian boxer, and De La Hoya defeated him easily. By the end of the first round, the judges' score was already 9-2 in Oscar's favor. Oscar knocked out Silva and won the first of five three-round matches. The second fight pitted De La Hoya against Moses Odion, a Nigerian fighter who lacked much style in the ring. Oscar defeated him easily as well, by a score of 16-4, racking up points for excellent punches.

In his third fight, Oscar faced Tontcho Tontchev, a Bulgarian. The match was unusually challenging, however, because the De La Hoya camp sensed that there was some corruption in the scoring system. (This was not the first time that Olympic judges had been suspected of dishonest scoring

Oscar's first fight on the road to an Olympic gold medal in 1992 was against Adilson Silva of Brazil. The 19-year-old De La Hoya turned in a performance of raw power, knocking out his opponent with seconds remaining in the third, and final, round.

of boxing matches.) After the first two rounds, despite landing several excellent blows against Tontchev, Oscar was shocked to see that he only led by a slim margin. At first, he wondered if the judges had been struck with temporary blindness, but then he realized he could be a victim of scoring corruption. He was furious. Surely, he had not come this far and trained so hard to be outdone by a political trick. De La Hoya decided that he would show the judges everything he had in the third round and make it impossible for them not to award him the victory.

In the third round, he attacked Tontchev so viciously that the score began to dramatically rise in his favor. He won the final round 9-1, and the entire match 16-7, much to his relief and that of his family.

His fourth opponent was Korean boxer Hong Sung Sik. Though he was shorter than De La Hoya, Sik was squat and built strongly. He grappled with Oscar in an almost wrestling-like fashion, throwing off De La Hoya's timing and boxing skills. "It was a terrible experience, a nightmare," he said later of the fight against Sik, which he always would remember as one of the toughest in his life.[19] Sik's fighting style lacked grace and style, but, it was powerful, and it caught Oscar off guard. Afterward, Oscar said, "I'd watched him earlier. I know how to box a guy who's in there to box, but I don't know how to box a wrestler."[20] De La Hoya finally rebounded and landed the punches he needed to earn the necessary points. The final score was 11-10 in Oscar's favor, barely a victory but a victory nonetheless. It was enough to move him into the final match, the one for the gold medal.

Oscar's opponent for the gold was the German boxer Marco Rudolph. Oscar had lost to Rudolph earlier in his amateur career. In fact, Rudolph was one of only a very few boxers who had ever defeated Oscar. Fully aware that he had previously lost to his opponent before, Oscar was very nervous stepping into the ring with him again, especially when every-thing was at stake. Early in the fight, the scoring and possible corruption once again worked against Oscar. After the first round, which he clearly dominated, the score was tied at 1-1. Oscar and his handlers were frustrated. It would be devastating to lose the gold because of shady, inside deals. Oscar decided he had to put everything he had into the next two rounds, and he did. He knocked down Rudolph to the canvas, but the German got back up. Yet, when the final bell rang, it was clear that Oscar was the winner, having dominated the fight from start to finish. Even Rudolph himself hugged and congratu-lated De La Hoya.

When the final score came in, 7-2 in Oscar's favor, Oscar dropped to one knee and remembered his mother once again. He made the sign of the cross and pointed upward to acknowledge that he felt her presence with him. He also put on a little show for the audience by dancing around the ring while carrying the American and the Mexican flags. This was to acknowledge and celebrate his dual heritage. After the exhausting fight, Oscar commented, "I'm very relieved now. All this pressure is finally off of my back. I was putting pressure on myself. 'I have to win the gold, I have to do it.' It's like a load off my back. Finally it's over and I'm happy."[21]

Yet, the pressure was just beginning for young Oscar De La Hoya. Now that he had earned a gold medal at the Olympics, he would turn professional. His gold medal victory had secured him the nickname Golden Boy, a moniker that would stick to him for the rest of his career. He would be a professional boxer and soon learn that the world of professional boxing was very, very different than the amateur ranks.

## PROFESSIONAL BOXING

Oscar's life was about to change in many ways. For one thing, he and his family moved to a better section of East Los Angeles. They bought a nice home in a safer neighborhood, one of Cecilia's dreams. Also, without realizing it, Oscar had achieved something else during the 1992 Olympics in Barcelona. He had become a television star.

NBC, the TV network that broadcast coverage of the summer Olympics, had zoned in on Oscar De La Hoya throughout the entire games. They had focused on the 19-year-old, handsome kid from the rough neighborhood of East L.A. and tracked his career up to that point. After all, it was a compelling story for NBC's television audience: here was a young man who had dedicated his life to training for the Olympics, still mourning the loss of his mother to cancer, and now in a foreign country battling against the world's top amateurs for the gold.

Oscar De La Hoya waves the flags of the United States and Mexico after his victory over Germany's Marco Rudolph to win the gold medal at Barcelona, Spain. The idea to wave the two flags was his mother's, in 1990, to honor both of his heritages.

Certainly, it did not hurt NBC's ratings that Oscar was such a good-looking young man who possessed movie star looks. Soon, people watching the Olympics back home in the United States knew the story of Oscar De La Hoya, and they were rooting for him to win it all.

After the final victory, when the gold medal was hung around Oscar's neck and the "Star-Spangled Banner" was being played, another type of contest had already begun. This contest would be to determine who would manage Oscar De La Hoya's professional boxing career. Everyone knew there was a lot of money to be made in the business. Oscar himself knew that he would be highly sought after, and those in his camp knew they had to play their cards carefully.

Although only 19, Oscar knew what was at stake. "A medal could set me up for life. It's kind of scary, because my life will change. There's a lot of crooks, people who just want to use you. Pro boxing is very dangerous, not only up in the ring, but outside."[22] The situation was more complicated because many managers and management teams had been courting the De La Hoyas for years, and now they returned to "collect." In the end, however, the De La Hoya camp settled on Robert Mittleman and Steve Nelson, a partnership that promised them the most money.

# Turning Pro

**It probably would have been fitting for Oscar De La Hoya to** make his professional debut in a world title fight. For a while, De La Hoya's managers, Robert Mittleman and Steve Nelson, considered the idea. The young boxer was full of confidence after winning the gold medal at the Olympics, and he badly wanted to challenge Genaro Hernandez for the World Boxing Association's (WBA) junior light-heavyweight championship.

A few months before the Olympics, De La Hoya pounded Hernandez in a sparring session. At the time, Hernandez was not in top shape and was doing De La Hoya a favor by getting in the ring with him and helping him train. De La Hoya was sure he could beat Hernandez again with a title at stake.

Mittleman and Nelson realized having a fighter begin his career with a championship fight was unprecedented. The mere idea of it displayed great arrogance on their part. Yet, it meant a big payday, and the managers knew they needed the money. Despite the strong temptation, Mittleman and Nelson, however, resisted the urge because they did not want to risk the possibility that De La Hoya could lose and start his career with a 0-1 record. In retrospect, Nelson later said:

> I'm not convinced he would've beaten Genaro in a first fight. Who knows, anything's possible . . . but to take that shot and lose would've been absolutely devastating. And we would've been called the stupidest guys in the history of boxing. I'm not saying he would've lost. But to make the first fight for a world championship, against a guy who's fairly well established. . . . You're talking about going twelve rounds before you even have a four-rounder.[23]

Instead of challenging Hernandez, De La Hoya's handlers settled on an easy opponent, Lamar Williams. Just like boxing legends Muhammad Ali and Sugar Ray Leonard, De La Hoya, the kid from East L.A., would make his debut in front of his home crowd at the Great Western Forum in Inglewood, California. During the weeks leading to the fight, Forum public relations director, John Beyrooty, nicknamed De La Hoya "the Golden Boy." He probably did not realize at the time that the name would stick with De La Hoya throughout his career. It was a perfect fit for the charismatic young man who had it all: talent, looks, and style.

A day before his debut, De La Hoya talked up his opponent. Williams was 7-2 with two knockouts in his brief career. "Lamar's never been stopped and he's never been dropped, so I heard he's pretty tough," De La Hoya said in Louinn Lota's article for The Associated Press (AP). "But most pros don't have what amateurs have in the ring. They don't have to think the way amateurs have to think." De La Hoya hated the clutching and brawling that some amateur boxers engaged in, and he was not fond of the computerized scoring system, either.

"In amateurs, the fight is over in three rounds," he said. "In professional boxing, you go much slower. You can take your time in six rounds, pick your shots. . . . I like working into the body, taking my time. My favorite is a hook to the body, and working back up comes naturally. I like confusing the fighter and using fast combinations."

Fight night was Monday, November 23, 1992. A crowd of 6,185, including new heavyweight champion, Riddick Bowe, watched the bout at the Forum. Of course, De La Hoya was the fan favorite. Some fans wore sombreros like the one on De La Hoya's head. Everyone cheered wildly when he entered the ring carrying Mexican and American flags in both hands and wearing a robe that was half-American flag, half-Mexican flag. A mariachi band played in the ring before the fight.

Once the bell rang, De La Hoya quickly went on the attack, according to AP writer Ken Peters's account. "He landed a barrage of blows to Williams' midsection and head and Williams crumpled in a corner. When Williams regained his feet, De La Hoya moved in again and landed more hard combinations. Williams made it up once more, but had nothing left," Peters wrote.

De La Hoya knocked Williams down just 48 seconds into the fight and did it again a few seconds later. Referee Marty Denkin stopped the fight just one minute and 42 seconds after it started. In a matter of minutes, De La Hoya was 1-0 without breaking a sweat.

Though it was only one fight, promoter Bob Arum sensed De La Hoya was going to be someone special. He envisioned making a huge profit on the kid, and he was not shy in the least about bragging to the world. "Oscar De La Hoya is going to be the biggest star in the history of boxing below the heavyweight division. Even bigger than Sugar Ray Leonard."[24]

## LOOKING FOR COMPETITION

Now that the first fight was out of the way, it was time to really start marketing De La Hoya. The best way to accomplish that

(continues on page 38)

# FIGHTING THE GOOD FIGHT

The fact that Oscar De La Hoya came from East Los Angeles, the country's most concentrated population of Mexican Americans, has been a source of pride for the Hispanic community. However, since becoming a celebrity, he has often had a difficult time with people in his former neighborhood. In some cases, the relationship has been a hostile one. Once, when he was marching in a Mexican Independence Day parade in Los Angeles, many people in the crowd that was composed of Mexican Americans, threw tomatoes at the stunned superstar.

De La Hoya was suffering the fate of being a true Latino crossover star, meaning that he is one of the first Hispanic-American celebrities to be loved equally by Mexican Americans and others of non-Mexican heritage. Mainstream America, for example, could not seem to get enough of De La Hoya, who was doing endorsements for major companies as well as appearing on the front covers of national magazines. At the same time, many Mexican Americans from East L.A. seemed to feel that De La Hoya had lost a sense of where he came from, the barrios, where his family first started out and struggled. He has been accused of being a sellout, especially for moving out of the old neighborhood or not taking the time to go back and visit old friends and acquaintances.

Yet, De La Hoya claims he is fiercely proud of his heritage. Many times, especially earlier in his career, he entered the ring wearing the colors of the Mexican flag and carrying a Mexican flag in one hand and an American flag in the other. After his Olympic victory, he said during an interview, "The American flag was for my country; the Mexican flag for my heritage."

Most recently, he has invested in several Hispanic-related business ventures, as a way to lend financial support to the Hispanic community. Plans for this venture include investments in health clubs, banks, and retail shops. De La Hoya claims he is undertaking these challenges by his desire "to really make a difference." When asked why he supported such ventures, he said, "It was an effort to give back to my community. I understand the Hispanic community. I live it. The projects will create jobs, create new businesses. It's hard to imagine the impact that it will have on people."*

In 1995, he established the Oscar De La Hoya Foundation to provide opportunities for East L.A. youngsters. The success of the Foundation has led to the creation of a state-of-the-art cancer treatment facility named the Cecilia Gonzales De La Hoya Cancer Center in honor of his mother, a high school, and a children's hospital, all for the benefit of underprivileged families. The De La Hoya Youth Center was also established to give kids in the community a place to go after school to focus on achieving positive goals. One of the activities offered is the boxing program for boys and girls ages eight to 18. Kids in the program are taught the fundamentals and discipline of boxing, with an emphasis on self-esteem. Team members get a chance to participate in competitions, exhibitions, and tournaments.

In 2003, De La Hoya made a donation of one million dollars to establish the Oscar De La Hoya Animo Charter High School in Boyle Heights in East Los Angeles. The school, managed by Green Dot, offers the youth of East L.A. a rigorous academic environment and aims to transform and resolve the educational problems that plague the Los Angeles public school system. The high school graduated its first group of students in June 2007.

In more recent years, De La Hoya hooked up with computer giant Microsoft to develop the Oscar De La Hoya & Microsoft Learning Center for the entire Los Angeles community. This worthy venture gives families in the region access to technology that will further education and communication, and improve the overall quality of life for those in the area.

* "De La Hoya, Battling Businessman." Business Week. Available online. http://www.businessweek.com/magazine/content/05_32/

Boxing promoter Bob Arum *(left)* is shown here with De La Hoya. Arum is a Harvard-educated lawyer who worked for the White House under President John F. Kennedy in the early 1960s. Arum has promoted many of boxing's biggest fights since the 1980s and, in recent years, has concentrated on promoting Hispanic fighters.

(*continued from page 35*)
was to find him better competition and to schedule a lot of fights.

The day after De La Hoya demolished Williams, Arum announced Oscar's second fight would be against Cliff Hicks three weeks later in Phoenix, at the America West Arena on December 12. The bout was on a Michael Carbajal undercard, billed as the Duel in the Desert, and would be televised on pay-per-view. Carbajal, the International Boxing Federation (IBF) light flyweight champion, was going against Robinson Cuesta.

De La Hoya's mind was set on winning a championship for his mother. "Winning a world title—that's my next goal," he said in AP writer Mel Reisner's article two days before the Hicks fight. "I can do that for my mother, too. She loved boxing, she loved to encourage me in the ring, and she was always with me, always supporting me. She wanted me to win a world title."

Hicks provided no more competition than Williams. De La Hoya knocked him down 40 seconds into the fight and finished him off with a straight right-hand punch just 75 seconds into the first round.

Two days after celebrating New Year's, De La Hoya was back in the ring. Again, it was not for long. He knocked out Paris Alexander in the second round at the Hollywood Palladium to improve to 3-0. De La Hoya dominated from the start, knocking down Alexander in the first round and twice more in the second to win the match. Yet, there was no time for a break. Mittleman and Nelson wanted to keep building De La Hoya's record, get him more exposure, and make more money.

Winning so quickly was somewhat frustrating for De La Hoya because he wanted to gain more experience in the ring. Also, he wanted to show that he could endure a long fight and hang in there against a tough opponent. He hoped his next opponent, Curtis Strong, could give him better competition in their fight at the San Diego Arena on February, 6, 1993. "Hopefully, it'll last six rounds because I'll get that experience that I haven't had before," De La Hoya said in AP writer Bernie Wilson's article. "We've brought in fighters who are quality opponents who have more fights than I do. It's a little frustrating for me having to train all that long and having it last two minutes, three minutes. But I'm not going to let that get to my head."

About a week before the fight, De La Hoya developed a cyst in his right leg. Yet, nobody wanted to cancel the fight because it was being televised, by ABC. De La Hoya had the cyst removed and did not let his leg affect his performance. De La Hoya, who had turned 20 years old only two days before the fight, bloodied Strong and won in the fourth round to improve his record to 4-0.

Manager Steve Nelson noted, "When he is in there, nothing is going to get into his way of winning the battle. He absolutely changes from locker room to ring. Intensity you can see in his eyes. I haven't seen it in anybody else's . . . maybe [Roberto] Duran had it in his heyday. Oscar's not playing the game, he's a changed man."[25] It was against Strong that De La Hoya took his first solid shot as a pro, according to Bernie Wilson's account for AP. "Strong backed him up with a double left hook," Wilson wrote. "But De La Hoya came back with a jab and regained control."

On March 13, De La Hoya made it five straight knockouts by wiping out Jeff Mayweather in four rounds in Las Vegas. Mayweather had only been dropped once in 27 previous fights and was expected to be De La Hoya's toughest challenge to that point. "But the lightweight from Montebello, Calif., treated Mayweather the same as his four previous opponents, wearing him down with hooks to the body and dominating the short fight," wrote Tim Dahlberg in an article for the Associated Press.

## GOING THE DISTANCE

De La Hoya's knockout streak finally ended when he fought Mike Grable in Rochester, New York, on April 6. Despite knocking Grable down twice during the bout, De La Hoya could not finish him off and ended up winning a unanimous decision in eight rounds. "I was hoping he would throw more punches so I could work on my defense," De La Hoya said in AP writer John F. Bonfatti's article. "I was just trying to pace myself more and look for that one-punch knockout. I was

De La Hoya's first true test as a professional boxer was against Jeff
Mayweather in March 1993. De La Hoya wiped out Mayweather with a hard
overhand right, followed by a crushing left upper cut. The victory raised
De La Hoya's record to 5-0.

trying to throw faster combinations, more powerful combinations and it did work. We were glad that it went the distance because we got to work more on our defense and get more experience out there."

More successes quickly followed. De La Hoya regained his knockout form in his next fight, dropping Frank Avelar in the fourth round on May 8 in Stateline, Nevada. Then, he improved to 8-0 with a first-round knockout over former International Boxing Federation featherweight champion, Troy Dorsey, on June 7 in Las Vegas. The fight was on the undercard of the George Foreman-Tommy Morrison heavyweight bout at the University of Nevada-Las Vegas (UNLV) campus arena.

Eight months into his pro career, De La Hoya was 8-0 and on a fast track for a world title fight. His handlers again had to decide whether it was time to challenge Hernandez for the championship or give him a few easier fights. De La Hoya earned $92,500 for beating Dorsey. Arum figured a title match against Hernandez would get De La Hoya a one-million dollar purse. Or, they could challenge John John Molina for the IBF championship.

After careful consideration, De La Hoya's management team decided to give him more time. Manager Nelson claimed, "We just felt it was more prudent to wait a little bit and not rush into it. In retrospect we probably should've taken it because [the De La Hoyas] were real anxious for the money."[26]

Instead of going for a title, De La Hoya made his first appearance on Home Box Office (HBO) television on the undercard of a Roy Jones Jr. fight in Bay St. Louis, Mississippi, on August 14. In that fight, De La Hoya knocked out Renaldo Carter in the sixth round for his ninth straight win. Two weeks later, in Beverly Hills, De La Hoya stopped Angelo Nuñez in the fourth round. De La Hoya was now 10-0 and really itching for a title fight.

First, he had one more tune-up, against Narciso Valenzuela, a light-hitting Mexican fighter who had lost 12 times in 49 career fights. The fight would be in Phoenix on October 30.

Valenzuela certainly did not stand a chance against the undefeated youngster. Yet, somehow, Valenzuela sent De La Hoya crashing down to the canvas with a hard shot in the first round.

It seemed the knockdown angered De La Hoya more than it hurt him, and it was a dangerous thing, most would agree, to make De La Hoya angry in the ring.

In *Golden Boy,* biographer Tim Kawakami notes, "De La Hoya hadn't ever been on the canvas, not in over two hundred amateur fights, not in the Olympics, not in his pro fights. He was stunned, but he wasn't hurt. He hopped right up from a seated position, winked quickly at Peralta [Oscar's girlfriend] sitting ringside, then glared intently ahead at Valenzuela, who seemed more surprised than De La Hoya by the development."[27]

When the fight resumed, De La Hoya attacked Valenzuela and immediately dropped him with a right hand. He ended the fight seconds later with a left hook. De La Hoya later said, "That was the first time in my career that my glove touched the canvas. It was a new experience. I guess it's sort of history—my first knockdown. But it's never going to happen again. I guarantee it."[28]

Now, De La Hoya wanted title holder Hernandez more than ever. He desperately wanted to be a champion. But his managers were concerned by the knockdown against Valenzuela. Perhaps, they thought, De La Hoya was not ready for the champ. Yet, before another fight could be signed, there was trouble brewing among the members of De La Hoya's team.

# Becoming
# a Champion

**Once De La Hoya took it on the chin and fell to the canvas** against Valenzuela, his managers crossed Hernandez off the list for possible next opponents. They simply did not think De La Hoya was ready to fight the champion. Therefore, Mittleman and Nelson decided to go in another direction. They wanted De La Hoya to win a title at 130 pounds (59 kg) before he grew out of that weight class. The World Boxing Organization's (WBO) super featherweight champion was an unknown fighter named Jimmy Bredahl, and even though the WBO title was not as important as the IBF's, a fight with Bredahl would serve their purpose. HBO wanted De La Hoya to sign a long-term contract to televise his fights, so the station agreed to broadcast the Bredahl championship fight. Before De La Hoya got in the ring against Bredahl, however, he was supposed to fight Jose Vidal Concepcion in New York in December.

While training for the bout against Concepcion, Team De La Hoya came apart. De La Hoya's father was so concerned about his son getting knocked down by Valenzuela that he persuaded De La Hoya's managers to bring in another trainer to assist Robert Alcazar. Manager Robert Mittleman chose Carlos Ortiz, a former lightweight champion. It was a decision Mittleman would soon regret, admitting, "I picked the worst guy in the world. An abrasive personality. . . . There were a million other guys I could've picked. . . . I should've just told the father, 'Hey, not now, we don't need anything now.' That would've been it. 'Alcazar's doing fine, it was a lucky punch by Valenzuela, Oscar got up and finished him right off.'"[29]

The situation got worse during a training session in which De La Hoya was hit hard because he was following Ortiz's advice and attacking aggressively. An angry De La Hoya cut short his third session under Ortiz and stormed out of the ring, tears running down his cheeks. He did not like getting hit, and he hated to get bruises on his face.

Alcazar, who did not like being pushed aside for Ortiz, comforted his pupil. That night, De La Hoya insisted Ortiz be fired. The next day, De La Hoya fired comanagers Mittleman and Nelson. Bob Arum remained De La Hoya's promoter. At the time, De La Hoya remarked, "They're all crooks and thieves. Bob Arum just is the straightest, nicest crook."[30]

De La Hoya canceled the fight against Concepcion, saying his hand was injured. Then it was time to face the cameras and explain his decision to fire his managers. At the news conference, De La Hoya explained, "First of all, they did not do what they promised in the contract. Breach of contract. They've breached the contract so many times. . . . We found out they had no money to support what they had to do. It was a very scary, very tough decision. But I put my foot down and that was it."[31]

De La Hoya also explained that his managers tried to manipulate him by aligning themselves with his father, who was supposed to control him. "My dad was scared. I mean, he was scared. They tried to get to my father because they figured, 'Oh, he has respect for his father."[32] The confident young boxer added, "My father will be behind me. Team De La Hoya will be back together. Robert [Alazar, his trainer], my brother, . . . Arturo (Islas, the cook), that's Team De La Hoya right there. The whole world will know what's going on, they will know I am a good guy. We have so many things planned. I mean, this is not all about money, this is about taking care of my family.[33]

Mittleman and Nelson, however, contended that it was De La Hoya who broke promises. "We're in complete compliance [with the contract]," Mittleman said in a telephone interview with the AP's Ken Peters. "They violated [the contract] before we did. He took a payment from us three weeks ago. He said he wasn't getting enough money. But he's already received over $800,000 paid to him in less than one year, out of $1 million supposed to be paid over two years. We made the kid a superstar. Now he wants to get out and kick us in the teeth."

With Mittleman and Nelson gone, De La Hoya turned to Mike Hernandez for guidance. Hernandez, who owned a car dealership and had given De La Hoya a Corvette for winning the Olympic gold medal, was a rich, proud man. He was also a shrewd business person. Hernandez provided sound financial advice and brought stability to De La Hoya's life.

De La Hoya eventually signed a lucrative contract with HBO that would give him $7.5 million for five fights with an option for five more that would push the total package to $20 million. Now it was time to win a championship.

## GOLD FOR HIS WAIST

De La Hoya's title fight against Bredahl was still on. The Golden Boy was an overwhelming favorite against the

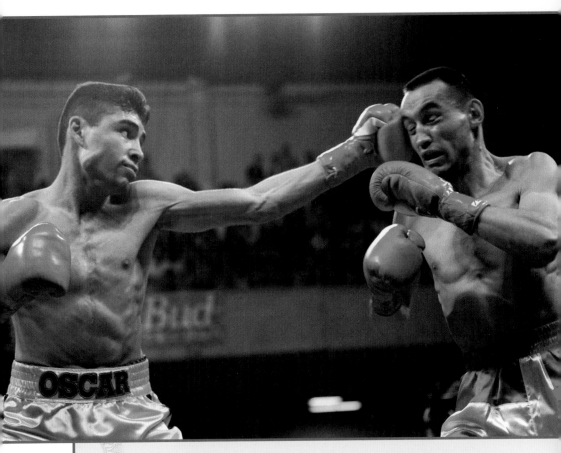

In March 1994, De La Hoya won his first championship, the World Boxing Organization's super featherweight title, by stopping Jimmy Bredahl in the tenth round.

defending champion. The fight was scheduled to take place at the remodeled Olympic Auditorium in downtown Los Angeles, making De La Hoya the third generation of his family to fight in the building, following his father and grandfather.

Because of the dispute with his managers, De La Hoya had not fought in five months by the time he faced Bredahl on March 5, 1994. There was no sign of rustiness, however. With the hometown crowd roaring wildly, De La Hoya knocked down the cocky Bredahl in the first and second rounds. Yet, Bredahl clutched and grabbed for survival and stuck around until the tenth round. Finally, the doctor stopped the fight. De La Hoya was a champion!

"Bredahl is a very good fighter and it was difficult to nail him," De La Hoya said in Ken Peters's article for the Associated Press. "He couldn't stand the pressure. I felt very strong, I was in command. I knew he would go down." Bredahl, who handed out invitations for a postfight celebration party before the match, gave De La Hoya credit. "I thought I was good; He's good," Bredahl said frankly. "My strategy was to kill his stomach. But he killed my face first."

## DEFENDING THE BELT

De La Hoya was a champion, but the WBO was considered a small operation. Perhaps it would be more impressive if

## THE GOLDEN BOOS

From the moment he captured the gold medal at the Olympics to fulfill a promise to his dying mother, Oscar De La Hoya became an American hero. He was a young, good-looking, superiorly-talented boy who rose from the gang-infested, poverty-stricken environment of East Los Angeles to become a world champion boxer. Everywhere he went, De La Hoya was embraced and showered with love—except for one night at the Los Angeles Forum.

A few weeks after successfully defending his WBO championship against Giorgio Campanella, De La Hoya went to the Forum to watch his next opponent, Jorge Paez, fight.

When De La Hoya arrived at the Forum, the crowd surprisingly booed him long and loud. It was quite a surprise, considering the fans were mostly Mexican and Mexican American. De La Hoya acted as if the jeers did not bother him. He even signed autographs for the female fans while their boyfriends hurled insults.

De La Hoya explained the fans' behavior, saying, "Since the Olympic Games, I've been the Golden Boy and this and that.

De La Hoya moved up in weight and won another title. First, he had to defend his super featherweight championship against Giorgio Campanella. The Italian fighter was undefeated at 20-0 with 13 knockouts. He was five feet, four inches tall, almost seven inches shorter than De La Hoya. Campanella was a heavy underdog against De La Hoya, who seemed more excited about fighting in the MGM Grand hotel in Las Vegas than being focused on his opponent.

Just 15 seconds into the fight on May 27, De La Hoya hit the canvas again. A hard-charging Campanella caught De La Hoya with a straight left to the jaw, sending the champ sprawling to the mat. De La Hoya got up at the referee's count of eight, finished the round off, and pulled himself together in his corner. He adjusted his approach and knocked

And now it's, 'He's this rich kid.' People want to see me go down. . . . You have to put on a good show because they pay the money. I'm going to do that, but I'm going to get my money and run. Of course, I want to win world titles and have a big name. But I want to have as few fights as possible and make the most money. My image is like a star image."*

The fans were booing the image, not De La Hoya. They resented the fact that he was so rich and so famous and that he really had not fought any legitimate opponent yet. Some Mexicans even considered him more white than Latino because he acted privileged and was protected all the time by those who surrounded him. Traditionally, Latinos favored fighters who were macho, rough-and-tumble brawlers, such as Julio Cesar Chavez. The fans also wondered why De La Hoya never went back to the old barrio neighborhood to keep in touch with his ethnic roots. Essentially, they believed De La Hoya was trying to distance himself from them.

* Tim Kawakami, *Golden Boy* (Kansas City: Andrews McMeel Publishing, 1999), 142.

Campanella down in the second round before finally knocking him out in the third. Afterward De La Hoya said, "I started out trying to be that big, macho fighter, bang with the great banger. By the second round, I realized that I could easily outbox him, get him from the outside using my reach advantage, and stay away from the left hook."[34]

Getting knocked down in the first round for the second time in three matches convinced De La Hoya to stop fighting at the 130-pound weight class. He had a difficult time maintaining that weight and felt unnaturally light and maybe even a bit weak. He had won a championship and defended it once. Now, he was ready to move on and up.

De La Hoya's next challenge was fighting Jorge Paez for the vacant WBO lightweight title. De La Hoya was thrilled because he could fight at 135 pounds (61 kg) instead of starving himself to make the weight at 130. Paez had far more experience than De La Hoya. He was 53-6-4, fighting 50 more times than De La Hoya. Yet, everyone on Team De La Hoya was very confident the veteran Paez would be no match, as trainer Robert Alcazar explained: "No question in my mind, Oscar's going to knock him out. How many rounds, who knows? It all depends on how many rounds it's going to take Oscar to catch him with a clean punch."[35]

Alcazar lost a coin toss, meaning that De La Hoya had to enter the ring first on the night of July 29 at the MGM Grand in Las Vegas. Paez, nicknamed the Clown for his colorful costumes and wild antics, skipped his usual zany entrance and headed straight to the ring. Once again, De La Hoya started slowly. This time, though, he did not hit the canvas. For the first time in his career, De La Hoya was not the crowd favorite, as the fans repeatedly chanted "Jor-ge! Jor-ge!" Paez supporters, however, did not have much else to cheer about that night.

Just 23 seconds into the second round, De La Hoya landed a flurry of punches, knocking Paez out with a left hook. Paez was counted out at 39 seconds of the second round and

De La Hoya won his second WBO championship, the lightweight title, in July 1994, when he knocked out Jorge Paez in the second round with a devastating left to the chin. Paez is also an actor and a circus performer.

remained on the mat for another minute. De La Hoya now had won two championships in two weight classes.

"I did not want to go out too fast because of what happened to me in the first round before. I did a lot of damage with my first few punches of the second round and that's when I knew I could knock him out," De La Hoya said in a Ken

Peters article for AP. "I wanted to put him out early because he had a lot of experience."

Paez had only been knocked down three times before and knocked out just once in his previous 63 fights. "I don't remember anything after getting knocked down," Paez said in Peters's article. "I don't remember the second round at all. . . . I've never been hit that hard by a punch before."

Team De La Hoya now turned its attention to Rafael Ruelas, the newly crowned IBF lightweight champion. Ruelas was born in Mexico but came to the United States as a child and turned pro at age 17 to support himself. It would take a while, however, to finalize a deal for the fight against Ruelas so De La Hoya stayed sharp by fighting Carl Griffith on November 18 at the Grand Olympic Auditorium in Los Angeles.

A confident De La Hoya promised he would walk home if Griffith landed even one punch in their fight. Griffith actually landed 13 of 95, according to one report. Yet, De La Hoya knocked him out one minute and two seconds into the third round to retain his championship and improve his record to 15-0. De La Hoya claimed he was "ready for the big fights now."

Still, he had to wait a few more months before he would face Ruelas, and so John Avila became next on the list. De La Hoya needed nine rounds to stop Avila at the Auditorium in Los Angeles on December 10. At one point in their fight, Avila stunned De La Hoya and forced him to cover up for almost a half minute. "[It was] nothing to be scared of," De La Hoya said in the AP's account of the fight. "I mean, I was in total control and he just made me move back a bit. But I can take a good punch and I know how to come back like a champion."

Now everyone was waiting for De La Hoya to fight Ruelas. Promoter Bob Arum, however, wanted it to coincide with the Cinco de Mayo celebration in May. So, De La Hoya had one more tuneup before the big fight. Juan "John John" Molina, a former IBF featherweight champion, moved up in weight class to challenge De La Hoya for his lightweight title. Molina, who had not lost in five years, was trained by Lou Duva. Both De La Hoya and Alcazar wanted to beat a Duva-trained fighter badly. De La Hoya entered the fight on February 18 riding a streak of 10 consecutive knockouts. Molina, however, was no pushover. The tough Puerto Rican took De La Hoya the distance, a full 12 rounds, and left the champion battered and bruised.

The judges awarded the fight unanimously to De La Hoya. Although he would have rather won early, De La Hoya finally got a chance to prove he could box 12 rounds, claiming, "I had to become a warrior. John John's more experienced, but I should've boxed more. . . . I fought a very unintelligent fight. But, with only seventeen fights, nobody in their right mind would've gone up against a great fighter like John John Molina. So you have to give me a lot of credit because I went up against a great champion."[36]

For the first time after a fight, De La Hoya had scars and wounds. His left eye swelled up and his head hurt. He did not want fans to see him looking weak and wounded. He vowed never to get hit like that again.

# 6

# The Big Fight

**Unbeaten after 17 fights with 15 knockouts, De La Hoya still** did not get enough credit because many critics thought he had not yet faced any stiff competition. Although he had already won two championships in two weight classes, De La Hoya needed to prove himself against a boxer who was not past his prime, or too small or undersized. Ruelas was the perfect opponent. He was only a few years older and a little taller than De La Hoya, and he had an excellent record of 43-1. Beating Ruelas could finally earn De La Hoya more respect from his doubters.

Team De La Hoya made several important decisions in the weeks leading up to the Ruelas fight. First, Mike Hernandez had De La Hoya hire a bodyguard named Eric Purvis to protect him from overzealous fans. Then, De La Hoya agreed he needed another trainer to assist Alcazar.

The De La Hoyas wanted a Mexican trainer and settled on Jesus Rivero, who needed to be convinced to take the job. Alcazar, however, resisted the idea and tried to keep Rivero away from De La Hoya. After two weeks watching De La Hoya train under Alcazar, Rivero spoke to the champion and instructed him he was doing certain things wrong. De La Hoya was interested to hear more, and he listened to Rivero's advice.

Biographer Kawakami noted that "as the camp wore down De La Hoya was visibly changing his style—fighting more fluidly, moving back and forth with his hips, easily avoiding hard shots and flicking inside and out for counterattacks—and it was fairly evident that he had altered his training situation. The sparring partners started telling outsiders that there was a strange little man doing most of the training, while Alcazar fumed."[37] It was Alcazar, though, who was in De La Hoya's corner on the night of the fight, May 6, 1995, at Caesars Palace in Las Vegas. Rivero watched in the crowd.

A minute into the fight, De La Hoya landed several punches. Ruelas stayed up, but got hit hard. A left to the chin in the second round sent Ruelas down, but he got up. De La Hoya knocked him down again, but Ruelas got up yet one more time. Finally, De La Hoya connected with repeated hard punches, and the referee stopped the fight. De La Hoya had his first non-WBO title. Now, he was the IBF lightweight champion too. The fight grossed more than $10 million in pay-per-view sales, more than several of the recent heavyweight bouts had made.

## THE RIVALRY

Now, three years into his pro career, it was time for De La Hoya to get in the ring with Genaro Hernandez. De La Hoya, who wanted to fight Genaro Hernandez for the WBA's featherweight title in his professional debut, finally got a chance to face his rival on September 9, 1995, at Caesars Palace in Las Vegas. A few weeks before the fight, De La Hoya uncharacteristically said, "I hate his [Hernandez's] guts. I've never hated an opponent more."[38] De La Hoya usually did not show this kind of emotion against an opponent. Instead, he would just confidently state that he would win and then got in the ring and did just that.

According to Kawakami, Hernandez was considered the "anti-Oscar," because he was "the fighter who received the raw end of the financial deal, who persevered the longest, and who was changed the least by his ultimate success."[39] Hernandez never moved out of the old neighborhood, and fans wanted to see him beat De La Hoya. Commenting on his opponent, Hernandez said, "I think the money got to him. I've got a little more pressure in this one, because a lot of people want to see Oscar go down, and they think I'm the person to do it."[40]

The bad blood between the two men and their camps had reached a boiling point, and now it was time to settle their differences in the ring. Hernandez did not tell anyone that he was fighting with a fractured nose suffered in a sparring session against "Sugar" Shane Mosley.

It took De La Hoya only six rounds to finish off Hernandez, who had trouble breathing through his injured nose. Hernandez simply quit. The two fighters gained a mutual respect for each other during the match and ended their bitter rivalry. De La Hoya then turned his attention to his idol, Julio Cesar Chavez.

## THE MEXICAN WAR

A De La Hoya-Chavez fight had been talked about ever since the Golden Boy had turned pro. The appeal was obvious. Chavez was a Mexican idol, and De La Hoya was the up-and-coming Mexican-American star. For a while, it appeared the two might not get the chance to meet in the ring, but Arum finally found a way to set up the marquee fight that everyone wanted to see.

Before facing Chavez, De La Hoya successfully defended his WBO lightweight title with a second-round knockout of

De La Hoya's manager, Mike Hernandez, convinced the young boxer to take up golf as a way of relaxing in his spare time. De La Hoya was a natural, and he loves the sport. He is shown here on the course in Palm Desert, California.

Jesse James Leija on December, 15, 1995, in his New York City debut at fabled Madison Square Garden. Mike Hernandez recognized the significance of the fight, saying, "I think if you don't go to Madison Square Garden you'll never be big. Madison Square Garden is number one for boxing."[41]

After beating Leija, De La Hoya was ready to move up to the light welterweight division and go after Chavez's World Boxing Council's (WBC) title. First, he delivered a beating to Darryl Tyson on February 9, 1996. De La Hoya knocked Tyson out in the second round to run his record to 21-0 with 19 knockouts. Now, De La Hoya-Chavez was going to become reality.

Chavez, the aging warrior at 34 years old, had just one loss in 99 career fights. He was the true Mexican hero, beloved in Los Angeles. Meanwhile, resentment for De La Hoya continued to grow in his hometown. While attending a parade celebrating Mexican Independence Day in East L.A., De La Hoya had tomatoes tossed at him from the crowd. Afterward, De La Hoya calmly commented, "They love me everywhere but L.A."[42]

Arum guaranteed almost $18 million in purses for the two fighters and set up a chaotic tour that would send both combatants to 23 cities in 11 days to promote the fight.

Once the tour settled down, De La Hoya and Chavez began training vigorously for their bout. During this time, De La Hoya and Rivero grew closer. The mentor and pupil bonded, with Rivero challenging De La Hoya to try to become a fighter that would go down as one of the greatest in history.

On June 6, at Caesars Palace, De La Hoya and Chavez finally faced each other in the ring. The crowd overwhelmingly supported Chavez, hoping the old warrior had enough left to beat the Golden Boy. Less than a minute into the fight, De La Hoya caught Chavez with a couple of quick jabs, opening up a cut above Julio's left eye that he had sustained in a sparring session. Kawakami reported, "His [Chavez's] face was a red river. A minute into the fight, De La Hoya was staring at an old, bleeding man, frantically and hopelessly wiping blood out of his eye, onto his nose, all over his body."[43] The bleeding continued for three more rounds as De La Hoya beat on Chavez. Finally, the doctor stopped the fight in the fourth round. It was Chavez's first knockout loss in 100 fights. De La Hoya had done it. He had conquered the Mexican king and captured the WBC light welterweight championship for his third different title in three weight divisions.

Downplaying De La Hoya's attack, Chavez said, "I was already hurt over my eyebrow. I really didn't want to postpone the fight because of it. . . . Oscar De La Hoya doesn't really have a big punch. I just couldn't see because of the cut."[44] When asked about Chavez's comment, De La Hoya shrugged it off, saying, "It shows that he's a crybaby. I'm happy because that means he can't take losing. He has to come up with excuses for losing to me."[45]

The cut, however, tainted De La Hoya's victory because it gave critics a reason to diminish his success against Chavez. Yet, it also set the stage for a rematch. Fight fans anxiously wondered how long the negotiations would take to make that happen.

## TAKING A BREAK

Soon after the Chavez fight, De La Hoya broke up with his long-time girlfriend, Veronica Peralta. (His family had never liked her very much, and the pressure had proven too much for De La Hoya, who already felt pressured in many other areas of his life.) De La Hoya also wanted to take a break from boxing for a bit and to do some golfing and enjoy himself for the first time in a long time.

Arum and Hernandez, however, wanted De La Hoya to quickly get back in the ring, build off the momentum of the win over Chavez, and capitalize on his growing fame. They booked a fight against Pernell "Sweet Pea" Whitaker, the WBC welterweight champion, for April 12, 1997. In the meantime, De La Hoya reluctantly accepted a bout versus former lightweight champion Miguel Angel Gonzalez, scheduled for November. A shoulder injury forced postponement of the

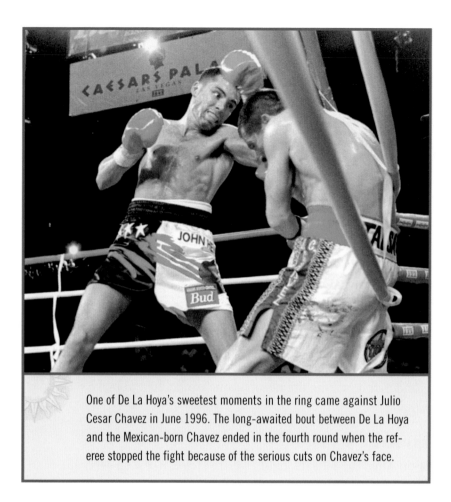

One of De La Hoya's sweetest moments in the ring came against Julio Cesar Chavez in June 1996. The long-awaited bout between De La Hoya and the Mexican-born Chavez ended in the fourth round when the referee stopped the fight because of the serious cuts on Chavez's face.

fight until mid-January, giving De La Hoya the time off he desperately wanted. The layoff helped him regain his passion for the sport, and he returned hungrier and more determined than ever. At the time, De La Hoya commented, "I have a love for the sport now like I had when I was six years old. The layoff was tough to handle. I missed fighting. . . . But I needed the break, too. Boxing is my number one priority now."[46]

De La Hoya appeared rusty when he faced Gonzalez. For the first time since he beat Molina, he did not have the killer instinct to knock out his opponent. He allowed Gonzalez to go the distance, before winning a unanimous decision to improve to 23-0 with 20 knockouts.

## HITTING THE LINKS

Oscar De La Hoya's manager, Mike Hernandez, convinced the young fighter to take up golf as a hobby. Hernandez thought that it would be a good way for De La Hoya to spend time outside the ring and enjoy nature while also making new business agreements with corporate executives who love being on the links.

De La Hoya agreed and decided to try the sport. After a few trips to the course, he was hooked. "He loved the culture—the wide open spaces, the male bonding, the pressure putts—and he loved the challenge of the game. Immediately, he talked about playing enough to qualify for the Senior Tour by the time he turned fifty, or maybe even the regular tour once he retired from boxing."*

De La Hoya joined Hernandez's course, the Friendly Hills Country Club, and played regularly. His promoter, Bob Arum, loved the idea too. It kept De La Hoya off the streets and away from trouble. It was also much safer than him playing other sports, such as basketball.

Boxing is a very different sport than golf. Fighters need to have a certain hard-core mentality to get into a ring against an opponent who wants to pummel them. Boxing is pugilistic and violent, but golf is passive and relaxed. Boxing is more of an inner-city sport. Golf is more popular among suburbanites. Yet, De La Hoya saw the benefits that golf offered. "I'm really into it. Because you can retire at fifty and go into the Senior PGA and still make a ton of money. It's just that the sport is very challenging. It's a mental game, you don't get hit, you can make money, get exposure, all that stuff. The golf course is where you don't get mobbed by people, you don't sign autographs . . . that's where you can go out there and focus and pay attention."**

    * Tim Kawakami, *Golden Boy* (Kansas City: Andrews McMeel Publishing, 1999), 159.
   ** Ibid.

Gonzalez, like Molina, had hit De La Hoya hard a few times and left him with some nasty welts. Tim Dahlberg's story for the Associated Press focused on the marks Gonzalez had left on De La Hoya's face, saying, "Oscar De La Hoya finally looked like a fighter, with his left eye almost swollen shut and his face marked from blows landed by Miguel Angel Gonzalez. And he [De La Hoya] was proud of it."

De La Hoya's approach against Gonzalez earned Rivero criticism. Members of De La Hoya's camp were getting irritated with Rivero because they considered him stubborn and too much of a talker. After the Molina fight, Alcazar was pushed aside for Rivero. Could it happen again? With the fight against Whitaker coming, De La Hoya could not possibly fire Rivero.

To fight Whitaker, De La Hoya had to move up another five pounds in weight class. The possibility that his power could be less effective against bigger fighters certainly existed, so now it was up to Rivero to ensure that De La Hoya could still knock out his opponents.

# Celebrity
# Status

Only two American athletes made more money than De La Hoya in 1997. They were basketball superstar Michael Jordan and boxing's heavyweight champ, Evander Holyfield. De La Hoya earned a staggering $38 million and was rapidly becoming a full-fledged celebrity. He had many endorsements, made numerous commercials, and frequently appeared on television.

In the ring, he moved up to the welterweight division for his bout against Pernell Whitaker, an Olympic gold medal winner in 1984 and the WBC champion. Once considered the best "pound-for-pound" fighter in the world, Whitaker was on the downside of his career. He was 33 years old and looking for a big payday. Whitaker knew how to get to De La Hoya, taunting him in the press and saying he wanted to hurt him in the ring. Yet, De La Hoya was hip to Whitaker's tactics, saying, "When Whitaker talks on TV and has all these interviews, it seems like he's a cocky fighter, like he can beat anybody he wants to. He was saying he was going to break my arms and break my chin. People don't want to hear that, they don't like that. Maybe the die-hard boxing fan gets a kick out of that, but the regular person is like, 'What kind of guy is this'?"[47]

De La Hoya and Whitaker met at the Thomas and Mack Center in Las Vegas on the night of April 12. Neither fighter took control in the early rounds, and it appeared Whitaker's southpaw stance was throwing off De La Hoya—until Oscar showed his secret strategy and began fighting left-handed in the fifth round.

The Golden Boy alternated left- and right-handed the next two rounds, but Whitaker's plan to stay away worked. De La Hoya could not knock him down. Still, he won the fight by unanimous decision and captured his fourth championship in four different weight divisions.

Whitaker and his camp complained that De La Hoya had gotten the benefit of charitable scoring from the judges, further proving that De La Hoya was viewed as superstar.

De La Hoya's relationship with his trainer, Rivero, however, took a dramatic turn for the worse because of the bout. He felt the strategy Rivero taught him was wrong for this fight.

"I think like in the third round, I said, 'Man, this game plan is not right.' It was hard for me to change. I won that fight on heart and talent alone."[48] Rivero never trained De La Hoya again, and he did not even get a phone call telling him he was fired. Veteran trainer Emanuel Steward was hired, and Team De La Hoya moved on.

Alcazar came back to assist Steward, and everyone enjoyed the first camp together preparing for a fight against David Kamau in San Antonio, Texas, on June 14. It would be De La Hoya's first time fighting in Texas, and he received a hero's welcome. Teenage girls flocked to him like he was a rock star. In the fight, Kamau proved no challenge. De La Hoya knocked

# CRASHING THE BENZ

Oscar De La Hoya was driving home from an awards banquet in an expensive Mercedes-Benz, speeding along the tight freeway, when suddenly he heard an unexpected sound.

The Mercedes, a $70,000 car, stalled out on the highway, and cars were speeding past. Panicked, De La Hoya desperately tried to maneuver the car to safety on the shoulder of the highway. "De La Hoya's heart raced. He started sweating, then flipped on the hazard lights, fearing a rear-end collision. He turned on an interior light, too, so he could be seen from behind."*

Yet, before he could steer the car onto the shoulder, he was rear-ended by a Honda Civic, whose driver fled the scene. De La Hoya got out of his car, ran across four lanes of the highway in the dark, and looked for a roadside call box. By the time he found one, another car had crashed into his Mercedes. If De La Hoya had stayed in his car a few more minutes, he certainly would have been injured—and possibly killed.

"I was just very fortunate I wasn't in there, but I'm OK," De La Hoya told KNBC-TV a day after the accident. "Now I know for sure that there is a God. If I was in that car 10 more seconds I would have been in it and just destroyed."

The near-death experience left a lasting impression on De La Hoya: He would not take life for granted anymore. "The accident just changed everything. I kind of saw how, if it all was over right there and then, what is my family left with, how is my family going to live?"**

After the accident, De La Hoya started thinking about marriage and having children. He even considered an early retirement after a few more years of boxing. Members of Team De La Hoya did not know what to think of the Golden Boy's new outlook on life. De La Hoya was maturing before their eyes, but they feared that by assuming new, more responsible roles, his desire in the ring would diminish.

* Tim Kawakami, *Golden Boy* (Kansas City: Andrews McMeel Publishing, 1999), 254.
** Ibid., 256.

The flashy, controversial Hector "Macho" Camacho was no match for De La Hoya in their September 1997 showdown. Here, De La Hoya lands a left to Camacho's head. Camacho was a three-time world champion with an impressive career record of 79 wins, five losses, and two draws.

him out in the second round for his first title defense as a welterweight. Steward had trained Thomas Hearns, Chavez, Holyfield, and Lennox Lewis. He knew his latest pupil was special, commenting, "Oscar's biggest asset I think is the unbelievable intensity and viciousness that he brings into the ring. He's totally transformed once the bell rings. And I have never seen a fighter who does that the way he does it . . . I just don't see him losing to anyone."[49]

Steward wanted De La Hoya to take it to another level and fight the best guys around. Beating a rising star like Felix Trinidad or perhaps winning a rematch against Whitaker could make De La Hoya the next Sugar Ray Leonard. Those matches would have to wait because De La Hoya's next fight would be against Hector "Macho" Camacho, a brash-talking showman who had fought many top-bill fights but was now moving past his prime. Before the fight against Camacho, however, De La Hoya experienced some ups and downs in his personal life. He got engaged but then called it off after finding out another woman was going to have his baby.

## SHUTTING UP THE SHOWMAN

As a boxer, the flamboyant Hector Camacho always enjoyed talking almost as much as fighting. The coming fight with De La Hoya was no different, as he boasted, "If I'd have met him when we were both 130 [pounds], I'd have killed him. On the streets, I'd have kicked his butt. But he'd never go to Harlem, anyway."[50] Camacho's trash talking made De La Hoya's camp think that he would be the perfect opponent against which to cast the Golden Boy in the "good guy" role, for once.

De La Hoya was a strong favorite going into the fight at the Thomas and Mack Center on September 13. He wanted to become the first man to knock out Camacho, who never went down for the count in his first 68 fights. Looking sharper than he did against Whitaker, De La Hoya dominated the fight. The Macho Man grabbed and held onto De La Hoya throughout the match, avoiding a knockout. A unanimous decision gave De La Hoya his twenty-sixth consecutive victory without a loss and left Camacho impressed. "Oscar is the best I ever fought," Camacho said in AP boxing writer Ed Schuyler Jr.'s story. "He did everything he said he would except knock me out."

De La Hoya immediately began talking about fighting Felix Trinidad and WBC super welterweight champion, Terry Norris. First, he had to face Wilfredo Rivera in Atlantic City on December 6. Before the fight, however, Steward became the latest trainer fired by Team De La Hoya, after the Golden Boy showed up at Holyfield's heavyweight fight against Micheal Moorer in November. Arum feared Steward was trying to set up De La Hoya with rival promoter Don King. So, he, Hernandez and De La Hoya's father decided they did not want Steward around any longer. "They were trying to find any reason to get rid of me. Everybody became uncomfortable with me—except for Oscar,"[51] Steward said. Alcazar regained his position as the top trainer, and Arum brought in veteran Gil Clancy from New York to assist him. De La Hoya knocked down Rivera in the fourth round of their fight and won it in the eighth round on a technical knockout.

After winning five fights in 1997, De La Hoya was ready for a break. He was supposed to defend his WBC title against number one contender, Patrick Charpentier, in February, but a wrist injury forced the bout to be postponed until June 13, 1998. Charpentier did not stand a chance against De La Hoya when the two finally met, at the Sun Bowl in El Paso, Texas. De La Hoya knocked him out in the third round for his twenty-third knockout in 28 victories. Now the pressure on De La Hoya to fight Trinidad or Ike Quartey or even to give Whitaker a rematch was building greater. Despite all his success, De La Hoya still had quite a few detractors.

### DE LA HOYA-CHAVEZ II

Tired of hearing Chavez complain about their first fight, De La Hoya chose to give the aging warrior a rematch instead of pursuing a more deserving opponent. De La Hoya wanted to prove beyond a doubt that he could beat Chavez. Plus, the fight was a lucrative one, and it would put De La Hoya over the $100 million mark in career earnings. The rematch was set for September 18 at the UNLV campus arena, with legions of Chavez fans hoping to see the Mexican fighter put up one last great battle. "This fight is a very personal fight to me. I'm fighting for the respect I never got beating him the first time,"

De La Hoya said in Tim Dahlberg's story for the AP. "If it were up to me, it wouldn't even be in the record books. That's how personal it is."

De La Hoya got his wish, beating up Chavez until the proud fighter sat on his stool and quit following the eighth round. For the Golden Boy, it was vindication, even though Chavez was 36 years old. "He beat me right," Chavez said in Dahlberg's article. "I told him this would be a great fight and he would get my respect. I give him my respect now."

Some viewed the fight as a sign that De La Hoya had flaws because the bigger De La Hoya got hit hard by Chavez several times. In *Golden Boy,* author Kawakami observed, "If Chavez could lean in, absorb the punishment and rock De La Hoya back on his heels at least two or three times, what would a legitimate welterweight hammer-hitter do to De La Hoya? What could Felix Trinidad do with openings like De La Hoya suddenly was offering? Or Ike Quartey, who was signed to meet De La Hoya in November?"[52]

De La Hoya was now 29-0, winning 24 times by knockout. Yet, it seemed the hard-core boxing fans still were not convinced of his greatness.

## SILENCING THE CRITICS

When De La Hoya signed to fight the undefeated Quartey on November 21, he hoped people would stop saying he was ducking tough opponents. "It'll stop the criticism a bit," he said in AP writer Beth Harris's article. "Chavez was an exciting fight, but this one is going to be a war. Hopefully, people will acknowledge the fact that I'm stepping up in talent with my opponents.

"Even [promoter] Bob Arum didn't want this fight to be next for me, but I wanted this fight . . . because challenges like these make me train harder and motivate me. I know that I'll be fighting all the fighters. I've just been very patient and it's sometimes frustrating that people in the media are not as patient as I am."

Quartey, from Ghana, was 34-0-1 with 29 knockouts. He was certainly a formidable challenger. "I wanted this fight for a long time," Quartey said in Harris's story. "I consider Oscar to be the best fighter in the world. He hasn't fought anyone like me. I don't think he can take my punches."

The fight was moved to February 13, 1999, because De La Hoya suffered a lacerated eyelid while sparring. The fight eventually took place, and Quartey proved to be De La Hoya's stiffest test to date, taking the champion the distance at the Thomas and Mack Center. Both fighters went down in the sixth round, and De La Hoya then floored Quartey again in the twelfth round. Yet, the challenger got up and finished the fight. De La Hoya was awarded a split-decision victory, the first time in his professional career that he did not win by knockout or a unanimous decision. "It was one of the greatest welterweight fights I've ever seen," De La Hoya's trainer, Bill Clancy, said in Ed Schuyler Jr.'s AP story. Schuyler also noted that De La Hoya "showed tremendous determination, especially in the last round."

For his part, Quartey was not pleased with the outcome. "I thought I did enough to win and I surprised him with my boxing ability," he said in Schuyler's article. "You know I couldn't win a decision in Las Vegas." For De La Hoya, it was a crucial victory. He had survived the hardest challenge of his career and remained undefeated.

With an eye on a megafight against Felix Trinidad, De La Hoya geared up for a bout against Oba Carr on May 22 in Las Vegas. A loss to Carr would ruin plans for the huge showdown against Trinidad, so De La Hoya had to make sure he was at his best. A day before the fight, De La Hoya vowed to revert back to being a puncher instead of a boxer. He did not like his cautious approach against Quartey and was not happy that four of his previous eight fights had gone the distance.

"I'm not boxing anymore. I'm going back to fighting, to the old school way," he said in Tim Dahlberg's AP story. "I'm going to walk through guys and destroy them. I guarantee you

Ike "Bazooka" Quartey, from Ghana, faced De La Hoya in February 1999 with an undefeated record of 34-0-1. De La Hoya won the controversial split decision to keep his WBC welterweight title. Many in attendance thought that the hard-hitting Quartey should have won.

there is no fighter in the world who can take my punch and last 12 rounds. So what am I doing boxing people? I should be going out there and destroying them."

It looked like it might be an easy night for De La Hoya after he knocked Carr down in the opening round. Carr, however, got up, and the two fighters went at each other for several rounds.

De La Hoya injured his left hand during the bout and avoided throwing jabs as much as possible. Yet, he used a left hook to send Carr to the mat in the eleventh round and gain that knockout win he had wanted so much. All that was standing in the way of a De La Hoya-Trinidad fight was Trinidad's IBF title defense against Hugo Pineda a week later. Trinidad made easy work of Pineda, knocking him out in the fourth round. The stage was set for the fight the world was waiting to see.

# 8

# Accepting Defeat

De La Hoya and Trinidad were two fighters with so much in common. Both started boxing at an early age and both enjoyed amateur success and became professional champions. Both packed a powerful punch, both had a loyal fan base, and both were main-event headliners. De La Hoya and Trinidad shared one more important fact: both were undefeated. It was a fight every boxing fan wanted to see, and it took archrival promoters Bob Arum and Don King to make it happen. De La Hoya would put his WBC welterweight title up against Trinidad's IBF championship at the Mandalay Bay Hotel in Las Vegas on September 18, 1999.

## WINNER TAKE ALL

"It's going to be a difficult fight, but I have a fighter's blood and I will not quit," De La Hoya said in Ed Schuyler's AP story three months before the fight. "On September 18, my fists will do the talking." Trinidad was even more confident. "I'm in the best physical condition of my life, and I can't see how De La Hoya could end the fight on his feet," Trinidad said at a news conference in his native Puerto Rico in early September. "I'm going to knock him out after the sixth round. When I put my hands on a boxer he falls, and De La Hoya will be no exception. He won't be able to take the punishment."

Billed as the Fight of the Millennium, the bout was expected to be an epic battle. Unfortunately, it did not live up to the hype. De La Hoya did not fight his usual, aggressive style. He was more cautious, wary of getting into a brawl with Trinidad because between rounds his trainers instructed him to box instead of slug it out. Still, De La Hoya dominated early on and led the judges' scoring through the first nine rounds. He landed several punches at the start of the ninth round and then started dancing rather than attacking.

Thinking he had the fight won if he simply avoided a knockout, De La Hoya took a very defensive approach following his final flurry. He backpedaled and tried to stay away from Trinidad over the last three rounds. The strategy backfired. One judge scored the fight a draw, and the other two favored Trinidad by a slight margin. The Golden Boy had finally lost for the first time in 32 career fights, although it was a controversial decision.

"I thought I had it in the bag," De La Hoya said in Ed Schuyler's AP story. "I swear I did. The 11th and 12th rounds, I was protecting the rounds I had in the bag. I was doing what I was trained to do—box. I landed a hundred more punches than he did." Trinidad credited his training crew for his success in defeating the Golden Boy. "My corner said keep attacking. I knew it was close. I put more pressure on him," he said in the AP story.

For several years after the fight, fans and experts still debated the true winner. Javier N. Perez, who analyzed the fight for Eastsideboxing.com, wrote:

Felix Trinidad, shown here shooting a jab at De La Hoya, dealt Oscar his first professional loss in 32 fights. In the September 1999 match, De La Hoya took a defensive approach, abandoning his usual aggressive style.

De La Hoya fans argue that Don King paid off the judges, and that De La Hoya exposed Trinidad as one-dimensional and provided the blue print that Bernard Hopkins and Winky Wright would utilize to upset him in future bouts. The Trinidad contingency replies that if Oscar hadn't been dancing around the ring Trinidad would have knocked him out, that De La Hoya felt Trinidad's power and was clearly concerned with being knocked out by his very worthy adversary and that it was this that the judges saw and what ultimately prompted them to give the nod to the Puerto Rican legend. Others argue that it was the ill-advice of De La Hoya's corner that drained this fight of it's drama and that the later rounds is not a reflection of De La Hoya as a fighter, but of the poor advice that he received from his trainers.[53]

Only a rematch could settle the argument, although De La Hoya made yet another change in his training staff because of the loss, firing Clancy and blaming him for the failed strategy against Trinidad.

## NO REMATCH

Negotiations for a rematch against Trinidad fell apart more than once, and, eventually, De La Hoya decided to move on to face other opponents. At a news conference announcing his plans to fight Derrell Coley on February 26, 2000, De La Hoya made it clear he was not going to chase Trinidad and beg for a rematch. "They made a wrong move by thinking they had all the power because they won the title," De La Hoya said in Schuyler's AP story. "They think I need Trinidad. I don't need Trinidad."

De La Hoya, still upset by the judges' decision in his loss to Trinidad, also promised to change his style against Coley. He wanted to get a knockout so there would be no dispute.

"I can't let the judges handle it," he said. "I'm coming out with anger. No more boxing. It's very sad people don't appreciate boxing anymore."

The loss to Trinidad only fueled De La Hoya's critics. The Golden Boy gave them more ammunition by pursuing a music career and getting involved in several endorsement deals. It seemed he was becoming too distracted by outside ventures to concentrate on boxing.

When it came time to get in the ring, De La Hoya still had the focus and determination of a champion. He showed it against Coley with a knockout in the seventh round of their fight at Madison Square Garden. De La Hoya dominated the fight, with only one judge scoring one round for Coley. Then, in the seventh, De La Hoya backed up his promise to be more aggressive. AP writer Barry Wilner wrote, "Coley attempted to pick up the pace at the start of the seventh round. But De La Hoya, 27, changed that strategy with a pair of jabs. Although he missed several wild lefts, he did get in a good left hook to the head moments before the decisive punch. That came as Coley was moving to his right, and Coley immediately dropped to the canvas."

The victory improved De La Hoya's record to 32-1 with 26 knockouts. More importantly, it was an excellent first step toward rebuilding his image as a power fighter. De La Hoya continued seeking a rematch against Trinidad but did not want to move up in weight class to fight him. Tired of the slow negotiations with Trinidad's camp, De La Hoya agreed to fight the undefeated "Sugar" Shane Mosley at the Staples Center in Los Angeles on June 17.

## A CHAMP AGAIN

De La Hoya's victory over Coley made him the WBC welterweight champion again when Trinidad had to relinquish that title after stepping up and beating David Reid for the WBA super welterweight crown. Now De La Hoya had to defend his belt against Mosley, who was 34-0 with 32 knockouts. The two fighters met in the ring once before, 16 years earlier. Mosley, who was 12 at the time, beat De La Hoya, who was 11. They also sparred a few times in 1992. This would be the real test, however.

With more than 20,000 fans watching, including many former boxing greats, De La Hoya and Mosley battled each other toe-to-toe for 12 fantastic rounds. Still stung by the criticism he received for the Trinidad fight, De La Hoya was intent on going for a knockout against Mosley. "Sugar" Shane, however, would not go down, and he earned the victory by a split decision on the judges' cards. After the match, a disappointed De La Hoya talked about a rematch but also mentioned the possibility of retirement. He and Arum were not pleased with the scoring, but it was not quite as controversial as the loss to Trinidad.

"I have to rethink my whole game plan in life," De La Hoya said in Kevin Iole's story for the *Las Vegas Journal-Review*. "This is a business, and of course people want the rematch to make more money. I don't see it that way. I'm thinking of my health and my career."

It was a defining victory for Mosley, who finally emerged from De La Hoya's shadow and captured the WBC welterweight championship after jumping up two weight classes. "In the 12th round, we went soul-searching to see who was the real champion," Mosley said in Iole's story. "De La Hoya showed he is a great champion. He stood there and fought with me for

## SINGER OR FIGHTER?

Oscar De La Hoya always dreamed of recording an album, but boxing always came first. The Golden Boy finally fulfilled his childhood dream when he released the album *Oscar De La Hoya* in October 2000. With songs in Spanish and English, *Oscar* was a huge success. It topped Billboard's Latin Dance charts for several weeks, and "Ven a Mi," a single from the album written by the Bee Gees, was nominated for a Grammy Award. The album itself was also nominated for a Grammy as best Latin Pop Album of 2000.

"I have been singing for a very long time, since I was like six years old, because my mother was a professional singer. . . . I kind of got the best of both worlds, the music and the fighting," De La Hoya said in an interview that aired on CNN on December 16, 2000. De La Hoya added that he drew inspiration from singing legend Frank Sinatra. "I grew up listening to Frank Sinatra a lot," he said. "He is like my little mentor in the music industry and I had the opportunity to [meet] him a few times and I've always looked up to him."

the whole 12th round. I whacked him a couple of times and he wobbled, but he stayed up and he still kept fighting. He's a true champion."

After losing to Mosley, De La Hoya had a new critic: Bob Arum. The promoter did not like the idea of his boxer recording an album in the months before he trained for such an important fight. "It was a stupid thing for him to do," Arum said in an interview with Fox Sports Network a few years later. "Boxing is a full occupation and requires tremendous focus. Oscar got diverted in his focus doing the album. I thought it was dumb . . ."

De La Hoya defended his decision, stating, "I had the opportunity to record an album or to train. I picked the music because it was kind of like the easy way out," he told the same

The decision to pursue a singing career and record an album while preparing for his first fight against "Sugar" Shane Mosley earned De La Hoya a lot of criticism. People speculated that he was not focused on boxing and that he was devoting too much time and energy into marketing himself and pursuing outside ventures.

De La Hoya, however, told CNN that his interest in music increased his passion for boxing. "I think the music, having to pursue that career and my dream, kind of helped out my boxing career so much because I feel that fire again, I feel that energy, where I just want to step inside the ring and really give it my all," he said.

Music critics praised his debut work. "The vocal ability is certainly promising, and the songs and instrumentation, if formulaic, are at the very least well-executed," said Adam Greenberg of All Music Guide. "So while the album is relatively unsurprising and uncomplex, it's not bad within its own little pigeonhole."

interviewer. "I didn't quit on boxing—I just kind of picked the one that was going to make me happy at the time."

## BACK TO BOXING

It took De La Hoya nine months to fight again after losing to Mosley. Once again, he had a new trainer. Floyd Mayweather Sr., whose son was the WBC super featherweight champion, replaced Alcazar and trained De La Hoya for his fight against Arturo Gatti on March 24, 2001, at the MGM Grand in Las Vegas. "Until now, he had pretty much been doing things on his own and he did a great job on his own," Mayweather said in Ed Schuyler's AP story two days before the fight. "Now I am teaching him what boxing is all about. If he did that good on his own, now that he has a good trainer, you are going to see a new and improved Oscar De La Hoya. I am teaching him defense and offense all together."

De La Hoya shook off the rust and stopped Gatti in the fifth round to earn his first victory in 13 months and boost his record to 33-2 with 27 knockouts. He graded his own performance a "C" and told reporters that he was dedicated to boxing more than a singing or acting career.

"I decided I want to box and give it my all," he said in Schuyler's story. "I can do my singing and acting after boxing . . . it'll only be a couple of years. I want no distractions. I don't want to think about anything but boxing." Of course, he also thought about a possible rematch with Trinidad or Mosley.

## A BOLD PREDICTION

De La Hoya moved up to the super welterweight class to challenge Javier Castillejo for his WBC title on June 23 at the MGM Grand. Three days before the fight, De La Hoya made perhaps the boldest prediction of his career. He vowed to retire if he did not beat Castillejo. "A loss would mean that's it, it's over," De La Hoya said in Tim Dahlberg's AP story. "I would have no reason to be inside the ring anymore." De La Hoya did

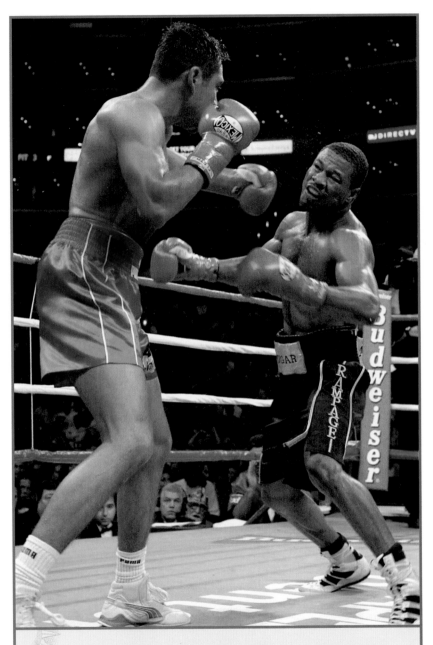

In June 2000, De La Hoya suffered his second professional loss, this one against undefeated Shane Mosley. For 12 exciting rounds, the two fighters battled, matching their skills and raw punching power. The final result was a split decision win for Mosley, who gained tremendous respect in the world of boxing after his win over De La Hoya.

not have to break any promises. He dominated the fight and scored a victory over Castillejo by unanimous decision to earn his sixth world championship in his fifth different weight division. Under the guidance of his new trainer, De La Hoya did not rely on his left-handed jab. Instead he offered more right-handed punches and power shots. "I mean Mayweather still has a lot in his arsenal, so we're just going back to the drawing board, and I'll come back with better stuff," De La Hoya said in John Gregg's article for boxingtimes.com.

# The End
# Is Not Near

**Every fighter has a bitter rival, someone they do not like** at all and want to beat badly. Muhammad Ali had Joe Frazier. For De La Hoya, it was Fernando Vargas. No one hurled more insults at De La Hoya than Vargas, a fellow Mexican-American fighter who also grew up in Southern California, also fought in the Olympics, and owned a share of the junior middleweight title. The similarities end there, however. While De La Hoya was the Golden Boy, Vargas was the street-smart tough guy. Vargas began the war of words by saying he was more of a Mexican than De La Hoya.

"[Vargas] is always talking about me. I think he's in love with me," De La Hoya said in a story written by Tim Graham for ESPN.com. "I actually hate the guy. I have never used the word 'hate' when talking about any other opponents, but I hate him." Vargas would not even consider losing. "I would rather die in the ring than lose to him," Vargas told Graham. "It's not about giving it a good try. For me, it's win or die trying. I'm going to do everything I can to make this the last fight of his career."

De La Hoya and Vargas got a chance to settle their feud in the ring on September 14, 2002, at the Mandalay Bay Arena. The fight was billed as Bad Blood, and the two boxers pushed and shoved each other at a news conference in January. It was a more civil atmosphere at the news conference the week of the fight, although Plexiglass screens were placed between the two men in case the situation got out of control.

On fight night, the fans roared loudly when the fighters entered the ring. It was quite a diverse crowd. "The fans of De La Hoya looking as if they were there for a Back Street Boys concert, the Vargas contingent looking as if they had just come from an Oakland Raiders game," Bert Sugar wrote on HBO.com. In the fight, Vargas outmuscled De La Hoya in the early rounds, but he could not deliver a knockout blow. De La Hoya, fighting for the first time in 15 months, gained the upper hand each time he could maneuver Vargas into the middle of the ring. Vargas rallied in the ninth and tenth rounds, but De La Hoya caught him with a left hook squarely on the jaw in the final seconds of the tenth round. Damaged by the shot, Vargas staggered to his corner. He came out for the eleventh round, but De La Hoya landed a flurry of punches, and the referee stepped in to stop the fight. It was vindication for De La Hoya, who captured the WBA light middleweight title to go with his WBC super welterweight crown.

"De La Hoya overcame questions both about his left hand and his ability to punch at 154 pounds to finally take apart a Los Angeles-area rival who did everything he could to irritate him," Tim Dahlberg wrote for AP. "De La Hoya needed to win what had become a neighborhood feud to set up two more fights he really wants—rematches against

Felix Trinidad and Shane Mosley, the only two fighters to beat him."

In April 2003, De La Hoya signed to fight Mosley five months later at the MGM Grand. The Golden Boy tuned up for the rematch by knocking out Yory Boy Campas in the seventh round of their fight in May.

## THE REMATCH

De La Hoya once again promised to retire if he lost to Mosley. He had so much going on outside boxing that he figured it would be a good idea to step aside while he still had his senses and good looks in tact. There was not any animosity between these two fighters. De La Hoya and Mosley had a mutual respect for each other. De La Hoya needed a win to avenge his first loss to Mosley and extend his career. Mosley did not have much success after beating De La Hoya the first time, losing twice to Vernon Forrest. A win would revitalize his career.

The Golden Boy came out strong and won the early rounds. Yet, Mosley put the pressure on and swung the momentum his way with a hard right to De La Hoya's chest in the eighth round.

Mosley outscored De La Hoya on each of the judges' scorecards in the final four rounds and earned a unanimous decision to capture the championship belts. The decision left the bloodied De La Hoya outraged. He even filed a formal protest with the Nevada Athletic Commission.

"It happened in the Trinidad fight and it happened here," De La Hoya said in Dahlberg's AP story. "I thought I won the fight. I didn't even think it was close."

As for his retirement plans, De La Hoya backed off those thoughts after the fight, claiming that he loved the sport of boxing and fighting like a warrior. He simply could not quit boxing, especially when he knew he was still capable of being a champion again.

## A CLOSE CALL

With retirement plans on hold, De La Hoya signed a lucrative contract to fight undisputed middleweight champion, Bernard Hopkins, on September 18, 2004. Both fighters had tune-up bouts on the same card in June at the MGM Grand. Hopkins

A CIRCLE OF FRIENDS

## THE DE LA HOYA CAMP

According to Oscar De La Hoya's biographers, it has been difficult for the young boxing celebrity to maintain a very tight circle of friends and confidantes. This is especially true when it comes to his personal trainers. The De La Hoya camp has seen many trainers, some who have become good friends of De La Hoya's, come and go regularly. Most of the time, the De La Hoya camp, which is composed of Oscar; his father, Joel Sr.; and other family members, made numerous tough decisions about who would best serve De La Hoya's career interests and goals.

One of these people was Jesus Rivero. In February 1995, De La Hoya hired Rivero as his trainer, and the older man came to be known as the Professor. Rivero's training philosophy clicked with De La Hoya, who saw the difference in the Professor's approach. Rivero's philosophy is that a boxer should not just be trained how to fight well but to be schooled in all areas and to develop himself as a person as well as a warrior in the ring.

Rivero believes, "A boxer has to understand things like music and literature and history and politics. He needs to concern himself with the great problems of society, of life. He needs to learn about history and economics. It's very important to understand the full world that's around him."*

It's easy to see why De La Hoya, who spent little time focusing on schoolwork because he was always so busy training in the ring, was attracted to the training theories of Rivero. He felt like he was learning a lot about life and developing as a person, not just as a boxer. Previous trainers had focused mostly on his fighting skills and finding easily won his fight over Robert Allen. De La Hoya barely survived against Felix Sturm, earning a unanimous decision to win his first middleweight fight and capture the WBO title.

"Everything went wrong tonight, everything. Everything went out, what can I say? I trained as hard as I can and we did

out how best he could win (and how they could get a share of his prize purse). Rivero, however, cared more about De La Hoya than about boxing records. "I think every boxer needs a man like this—a professor," Oscar said of Rivero. "This guy brings out the best in you."**

Their relationship, however, did not last very long. Two years later, when De La Hoya started to show slight signs of struggle in the ring, although he was still winning, his camp decided to fire Rivero. They turned to Robert Alcazar, a family friend and off-again, on-again trainer who had previously worked with De La Hoya. Alcazar had joined the De La Hoya camp shortly before Oscar had set his sights on the Olympics, when he was still an amateur. He had hung around in the sidelines, giving advice and helping out when he could. In 1991, however, the De La Hoyas made Alcazar Oscar's main trainer.

Nevertheless, Alcazar's relationship with De La Hoya would be a rocky one. The same is true with most of those in the De La Hoya circle. Most recently, his trainer was Freddie Roach, a former boxer who prepared him for the Mayweather fight in May 2007. Roach was one of boxing's most sought-after trainers, having trained 18 world champions. Roach, a former fighter himself, was elected to the World Boxing Hall of Fame as a trainer and was once selected Trainer of the Year. Yet, after De La Hoya's defeat, it remains uncertain if Roach will stay on with the De La Hoya team.

   \*   Tim Kawakami, *Golden Boy* (Kansas City: Andrews McMeel Publishing, 1999), 236.

\*\*   Ibid., 237.

everything perfect, sparring with big guys but I stepped in the ring and boom," De La Hoya said about the bout with Sturm in John Gregg's story for boxingtimes.com. "He's an ordinary fighter. I mean he's a world champion and he's young and he's hungry and I give him all the respect in the world. But I know in my heart I can do better." Sturm, a German fighting in the United States for the first time, protested the fight, claiming the judges were influenced by the high stakes of the coming De La Hoya-Hopkins fight.

## THE DEFINING FIGHT

Twelve years after turning pro at 130 pounds, De La Hoya was fighting for the middleweight championship at 158 pounds (972 kg). Hopkins, his older opponent, had not lost in 11 years and was a 2-to-1 favorite to successfully defend his titles. The odds were stacked against De La Hoya, who faced a bigger and stronger opponent for the first time. The two men could not be more different. Hopkins once served a prison sentence and overcame several obstacles to become a champion. The differences were underscored by Tim Dahlberg of the AP when he wrote, "De La Hoya brings big fight experience and a glittering reputation into the ring. Hopkins carries with him a hunger born out of scrapping for every dollar he could get."

Though he was 39 years old, Hopkins was out to prove he was the best fighter in the world. De La Hoya wanted to repair his image, which was tarnished by two losses to Mosley and one to Trinidad. Often criticized for choosing opponents past their prime or vulnerable, De La Hoya gained some respect for taking on a formidable foe. "This is the fight where I just suck it up and let everything loose," De La Hoya said in Dahlberg's AP story. "This is for all the marbles. This is the fight that will define my career."

Entering the ring to Frank Sinatra's "My Way," Hopkins had a fierce look of determination on his face. De La Hoya, however, would not be intimidated. He surprised boxing analysts by standing toe-to-toe in the middle of the ring and

In September 2004, Bernard "the Executioner" Hopkins became the first man to knock out Oscar De La Hoya. Hopkins was defending his WBC, WBA, and IBF middleweight titles against WBO champion De La Hoya. It was Hopkins's sharp left hook to De La Hoya's ribs in the ninth round that ended the fight.

trading punches with Hopkins, instead of using his speed and quickness to make the champion chase him. By the ninth round, De La Hoya had swelling and bruising around both of his eyes. Still, he was going after Hopkins and had a chance to win. Then, his dream suddenly collapsed. A perfectly placed left hook to his liver sent De La Hoya to the canvas, writhing in pain and pounding the mat in frustration.

For the first time in his career, the Golden Boy did not get up. Everyone was stunned. Hopkins became the first man to knock out Oscar De La Hoya. "He got me right on the button," De La Hoya said in John Gregg's story for boxingtimes.com. "Believe me, I tried getting up but I couldn't. I have what it takes, but he hit me right on the button."

De La Hoya, who made more than $30 million for the fight, said it would define his career. He would never forget the feeling of being knocked out, down on the mat, and unable to get up. Afterward, he had to deal with the fact that he came up short in some of his biggest fights. "I feel proud but obviously very disappointed, but I don't regret it at all," he said.

## A LONG BREAK

De La Hoya did not retire after his loss to Hopkins, but he took off 20 months before returning to the ring, this time against Ricardo Mayorga. Many questioned De La Hoya's motivation for staying in boxing. He had earned plenty of money, won several championships, and earned a place in boxing history among the elite fighters. Even his company, Golden Boy Promotions, was thriving. Yet, boxing still was in De La Hoya's blood. He was not ready to let it go, even though he now was 33 years old.

The layoff did not affect De La Hoya, who was cheered loudly at the MGM Grand as he dominated Mayorga in their fight on May 6, 2006. De La Hoya stopped the Nicaraguan brawler in the sixth round to claim the WBC super welterweight title and put himself in a position to retire on top.

Immediately after the fight, however, Floyd Mayweather Jr. issued a challenge to De La Hoya. "If Oscar wants to go out on top being the best, I believe on Sept. 16 we must meet," Mayweather said in Tim Dahlberg's AP story. "It's about legacy." It took six months for the two sides to reach an agreement. Instead of retiring as champion, De La Hoya signed to put his title on the line against Mayweather on May 5, 2007, at the MGM Grand.

## THE FINAL FIGHT?

A victory over Mayweather, widely considered the best pound-for-pound fighter in the world, would have been a perfect ending to De La Hoya's brilliant career. To ensure there would be no distractions, De La Hoya replaced Floyd Mayweather Sr. with Freddie Roach as his trainer in late January. Even though the father and son Mayweathers were feuding, De La Hoya was not comfortable with the situation. "I really didn't feel he [Mayweather senior] was going to be as passionate as I'm going to be," De La Hoya told reporters in a conference call from Puerto Rico.

"How is he going to feel when we're in the middle of training camp and some of his family members call him and say, 'Don't do it.' I don't want [any] distractions. This is the fight of my life."

The hype for this big fight exceeded any in recent years. HBO ran a reality show series titled "24/7." De La Hoya and Mayweather also went on an 11-city tour to promote the event.

"This is a fight where maybe it could solidify my legacy," De La Hoya said, when the tour reached New York City in February. "I want to close that book with a happy ending."

The talkative Mayweather, nicknamed the Pretty Boy, hardly let De La Hoya get a word in on the tour. "I'm the top dog in the sport," he said. "Come May 5, when I touch you, you're going to hurt for a week. And believe me, I'll give you something to cry about."

Once again, the crowd was pro-De La Hoya, as he battled against boxing's latest bad boy, Mayweather Jr. They roared with every punch De La Hoya threw. The two fighters battled each other for 12 rounds, neither of them going down or seeming to get hurt badly. De La Hoya delivered more punches, but

In one of boxing's most hyped fights ever, Floyd Mayweather Jr. defeated De La Hoya in a super welterweight showdown in May 2007. The undefeated Mayweather won a split decision over De La Hoya to take his WBC title.

Mayweather's slippery defensive tactics allowed him to move out of harm's way quite a bit. In the final round, De La Hoya got the slugfest he wanted.

The fight ended with the both boxers wildly trading punches until the bell rang. Then it was time for the judges to decide. Once again, however, De La Hoya was on the losing end of a split decision. Mayweather claimed the fight was easy work for him, proclaiming that De La Hoya could not "beat the best."

Ironically, Mayweather Sr. sat ringside watching the fight in seats provided for him by De La Hoya. He thought his son had lost, commenting that De La Hoya won the fight on points, had thrown more punches, and was more aggressive. The elder Mayweather complimented his son's efforts but still thought that De La Hoya fought well enough to win the fight.

This time, De La Hoya did not argue with the slim margin of defeat, telling reporters, "You just have to respect the judges at this point," he said. "I don't feel like a loser, because I came to do what I had to do. Now, as a champion, he has a big responsibility to work harder and maintain that title."

The fight set a record for most televised buys, surpassing Mike Tyson's second fight with Evander Holyfield and making it boxing's richest event. A total of 2.15 million households paid $54.95 to watch the fight, which generated revenue of $120 million. The previous record set by Tyson-Holyfield was 1.99 million buys. The Associated Press reported De La Hoya earned $45 million and Mayweather made more than $20 million.

Though his record fell to 38-5, De La Hoya proved he was still boxing's biggest draw.

Would he fight again? "I'm going to be very smart about the situation," De La Hoya said. "I will go home and watch the fight and see how my movements were, how my body reacted, and analyze the situation. I'll wait and see. I'll analyze the whole thing and think about it." Even if he never stepped into a ring again, De La Hoya was certain to be remembered as one of the greatest champions in boxing history.

# 10

# Family Man

**Fame and celebrity had brought Oscar De La Hoya something** that he had never expected when he was a young kid running away from fights and conflicts: a reputation as a ladies' man. Because of his good looks and rising career as a boxer, De La Hoya found out that it was easy to have women trailing him everywhere he went. At every fight and public event featuring De La Hoya, women could be found scrambling for his autograph, throwing him their phone numbers, and even trying to kiss him. He shrugged off most of the attention, but he did get into several brief relationships that have only cemented his reputation as a ladies man.

Between 1998 and 1999, De La Hoya had at least three children, whom he acknowledged as his own. Their mothers were actress Shanna Moakler, showgirl Angelicque McQueen, and a woman who has kept her identity unknown to the public

Oscar and wife, Millie Corretjer *(right)*, were married in 2001. Corretjer hosted a television show in Puerto Rico as a teenager and has released several albums. Her soft, angelic singing voice has made her a well-known performer in Puerto Rico.

to protect her privacy. There was another case, in which De La Hoya was accused of assaulting a woman, but the case was settled out of court. Also, De La Hoya had been engaged briefly to another young woman, though the relationship ended rather quickly.

*(continues on page 98)*

## A TRUE CHAMPION?

Oscar De La Hoya will long be remembered for his many contributions to the people and neighborhoods of Los Angeles, especially in the Eastside. The foundations he has established will create jobs, and new businesses and opportunities, which, it is hoped, will revitalize entire neighborhoods. The health facilities, schools, and learning centers that he sponsors offer young people the prospect of better futures for themselves and their families. De La Hoya has cemented his legacy as someone who cares for others and is willing to work on their behalf. Yet, what of De La Hoya's legacy as a *boxer*? How will future generations of fight fans judge his performance in the ring against the boxing greats of all-time?

The list of De La Hoya's accomplishments in the ring is nothing short of amazing. Working his way through the amateur ranks, De La Hoya amassed a stunning record of 223 wins (163 by knockout) and only five losses. He capped off that career with a gold medal victory in the 1992 Olympics in Barcelona, Spain. Even before the big win in Barcelona, De La Hoya, in 1990, had captured gold medals in the U.S. National Championships, the Goodwill Games, and in the U.S. Olympic Cup. After he turned pro in 1992, De La Hoya won six professional titles in six different weight divisions: super featherweight, lightweight, super lightweight, welterweight, junior middleweight, and middleweight.

In 1995, he was selected *Ring Magazine*'s Fighter of the Year. *Ring Magazine*, the "bible" of the fight world, honored De La Hoya two years later by selecting him as the best "Pound for Pound" boxer in the world. His professional record stands at a brilliant 38 wins (30 by knockout) and only five losses.

Yet, aside from the numbers, De La Hoya had always gone up against the best fighters of his generation in the 135-pound to 160-pound classes. The list of opponents is impressive and includes Rafael Ruelas, Juan Molina, Felix Trinidad, Genaro Hernandez, Shane Mosley, and Floyd Mayweather Jr., among many others. Few fighters in the history of boxing have faced a list of foes with such depth and range of competition.

Some critics, however, have slammed De La Hoya for a number of reasons. First, they claim, he was not the best fighter of his generation because he lost almost as many "big" fights as he won. De La Hoya is also criticized for not being the best-conditioned fighter in boxing because he often got tired in the latter stages of his bouts. Another criticism claims that he relied too heavily on his devastating left hand, suggesting that he was not a "complete" fighter.

Yet, as Yahoo! boxing writer Kevin Iole pointed out in May 2007, prior to De La Hoya's battle against Mayweather, "He [De La Hoya] unquestionably is the single most important figure in the fight game of the last 15 years."* Because of his popularity and his ability to generate millions and millions of dollars in the ring, "De La Hoya is the game's largest draw and has the ability to dictate who he fights, where he fights and when he fights,"** Iole added.

As he entered the later stages of his career, De La Hoya could simply have chosen to fight easy opponents, running up his won-lost record and making millions of more dollars by knocking out mediocre foes. Yet, he chose not to—a testament to his integrity and good character. In fact, De La Hoya fought Mayweather in 2007, when that younger opponent was at the peak of his ability, and De La Hoya was clearly not in his prime. This willingness to fight anyone and remain aggressive in the ring are trademarks of enduring champions.

De La Hoya remained at the top of his game for more than 10 years, far longer than most boxers do. During that time, he had been a goodwill ambassador for the sport, always in the role of gentleman, always accessible to his fans and the media, and always willing to take on the best there was.

As Sportstar Weekly! commented in July 2007, "De La Hoya will leave a positive legacy as a fighter and for this he must be saluted."***

   *  Kevin Iole. "Oscar's Legacy." Yahoo Sports! Available online at http://sports.yahoo.com/box/news?slug=kioscar050507&prov=yhoo&type=l gs

  **  Ibid.

*** "De La Hoya: What Next?" Sportstar Weekly! Available online at http://

(*continued from page 95*)

In 2001, however, it seemed that the Golden Boy had settled down. While he was recording his album, *Oscar,* he met Millie Corretjer, a singer from Puerto Rico who had several albums of her own. Millie had been a singing sensation as a young woman and received a record deal with EMI Latin at the age of 18. Since that time, for the last nine years, she had been recording songs and albums. She was beautiful, and De La Hoya and his producers wanted her to star in one of his videos from the album. She agreed, and the rest is history. In 2001, the couple married. Corretjer was 27 and De La Hoya was 28.

In an interview with *Parade Magazine,* De La Hoya recalled that Millie Corretjer was not really aware who he was when they met. In fact, she knew very little about American boxing. "She didn't like the sport and didn't even know who I was when we met," he said. "But, gradually, she became my biggest fan."[54]

The wedding took place in Puerto Rico. The bride and groom wanted to ensure their privacy, so the wedding was kept as secret as possible, and no media were permitted to be present. Some Spanish papers reported that the bride and groom were even covered by a large sheet to prevent photographers from snapping photos of the couple.

The couple owns a home in Los Angeles, but they spend a lot of time in Puerto Rico, where they also own a large home. In 2005, Millie gave birth to their son, Oscar Gabriel De La Hoya. One hour after De La Hoya lost the much-touted fight to Floyd Mayweather Jr. in 2007, Millie helped lighten the burden he felt by revealing to him that she was pregnant with their second child. "I think tonight is a good night to tell him," she said to a reporter from the *Los Angeles Times.* "He has a lot to look forward to now."[55]

She also revealed that she hopes De La Hoya will consider retiring from boxing. It is not certain whether he will or not, but one thing is sure. Between his business endeavors, charity work, and growing family, the Golden Boy will have

De La Hoya was honored by his hometown when the city proclaimed October 3, 2002, "Oscar De La Hoya Day" in Los Angeles. His brother, Joel Jr. *(far left)* and promoter Bob Arum *(far right)* join Oscar in the celebration.

a lot to keep him busy. Most recently, De La Hoya's side as a "family man" has been developing. In 2006, he co-authored a children's book, entitled *Super Oscar,* based on his own childhood memories. The book was released in a bilingual edition, Spanish and English, to appeal to a wider market. He had also been pursuing business deals, many aimed at helping to boost the Latin-American community.

The long road from his East L.A. barrio to the pinnacle of success as a world champion professional boxer has been a long and often difficult journey for Oscar De La Hoya. Without question, however, is the great legacy he leaves behind as one of the sport's most talented and successful giants.

# Chronology

1973    Oscar De La Hoya, the second son of Joel Sr. and Cecilia De La Hoya, is born in East Los Angeles on February 4.

1979    Begins training at the Eastside Boxing Club.

1990    Wins the gold medal in the U.S. National Championships.

1992    Wins the Olympic gold medal in Barcelona, Spain.

1992    Ends his amateur career with a record of 223 wins, 163 by knockout, and five losses.

1992    Makes his professional debut as a boxer; wins four titles in four separate weight divisions.

1995    Named "Fighter of the Year" by *Ring Magazine.*

1996    De La Hoya accused of assaulting a woman, with whom he later makes a settlement and avoids a trial.

1973
Oscar De La
Hoya is born
on February
4 in East Los
Angeles

1992
Wins the gold
medal in sum-
mer Olympics
in Barcelona,
Spain; makes
professional
boxing debut

1999
Loses bouts to
Felix Trinidad
and "Sugar"
Shane Mosley

# 1973

# 1999

1990
Wins the gold in
the U.S. National
Championships

1995
Named
"Fighter of the
Year" by *Ring
Magazine*

**1997** Named best "Pound-for-Pound" fighter by *Ring Magazine.*

**1998** Son, Jacob, is born on February 18; mother's identity is unknown.

Son, Devon, is born on November 30; mother is Angelicque McQueen.

**1999** Daughter, Atiana Cecilia, is born on March 29; mother is Shanna Moakler.

**1999** Loses to Felix Trinidad and "Sugar" Shane Mosley.

**2000** Releases a music album of Spanish songs, *Oscar De La Hoya;* album is nominated for a Grammy Award.

**2001** Marries singer Millie Corretjer of Puerto Rico.

**2002** Fights "Ferocious" Fernando Vargas, his nemesis, and defeats him by knockout.

**2000**
Releases a music album of Spanish songs, entitled *Oscar De La Hoya*

**2004**
Becomes first boxer in history to win world titles in six different weight divisions

**2000**

**2007**

**2001**
Marries singer Millie Corretjer of Puerto Rico

**2007**
Loses a much-touted and highly publicized fight against Floyd Mayweather Jr.

**2003** Loses the world title to Shane Mosley.

**2004** Wins fight against Felix Sturm for world middleweight title and becomes first boxer in history to win world titles in six different weight divisions.

Hosts and stars in *The Next Great Champ*, a reality TV show about boxing, on the Fox Network.

**2005** De La Hoya and Corretjer's son, Oscar Gabriel, is born on December 29.

**2007** Loses a much-touted and highly publicized fight against Floyd Mayweather Jr.

# Notes

**Chapter 1**

1 Tim Kawakami, *Golden Boy* (Kansas City: Andrews McMeel Publishing, 1999), 57.
2 Ibid.
3 Ibid., 59.
4 Ibid., 60.

**Chapter 2**

5 Ibid., 19.
6. Ibid., 18.
7 Ibid., 24.
8 "Oscar De La Hoya." Latino Sports Legends. Available online at http://www. latinosportslegends.com/ Delahoya_Oscar_bio.htm.
9 Kawakami, 27.
10 Ibid., 29.

**Chapter 3**

11 Ibid., 31.
12 Ibid., 35.
13 Ibid., 38.
14 Ibid., 42.
15 Ibid., 39.
16 Ibid.
17 Ibid., 62.
18 Ibid., 63–64.
19 Ibid., 74.
20 Ibid., 76.
21 Ibid., 80.
22 Ibid., 65.

**Chapter 4**

23 Ibid., 102.
24 Ibid., 105.
25 Ibid., 106.
26 Ibid., 107.
27 Ibid., 113.
28 Ibid., 113–114.

**Chapter 5**

29 Ibid., 116.
30 Ibid., 120.
31 Ibid., 123.
32 Ibid.

33 Ibid., 123–124.
34 Ibid., 140.
35 Ibid., 144.
36 Ibid., 155.

**Chapter 6**

37 Ibid., 170.
38 Ibid., 179.
39 Ibid., 180.
40 Ibid., 182.
41 Ibid., 224.
42 Ibid., 226.
43 Ibid., 242.
44 Ibid., 246.
45 Ibid.
46 Ibid., 260.

**Chapter 7**

47 Ibid., 267.
48 Ibid., 274.
49 Ibid., 288.
50 Ibid., 294–295.
51 Ibid., 300.
52 Ibid., 308.

**Chapter 8**

53 Javier Perez. "Oscar De La Hoya vs. Felix Trinidad: A Fight Frozen In Time." East Side Boxing. Available online at http://www.eastsideboxing.com/ news.php?p=7543&more=1.

**Chapter 10**

54 James Brady. "In Step with Oscar De La Hoya." Parade. Available online at http://www.parade. com/articles/editions/2007/ edition_04-22-2007/In_Step_ With…Oscar_de_la_Hoya.
55 Sara Hammel. "Oscar De La Hoya to Be a Father—Again." People Magazine Online. Available online at http:// www.people.com/people/ article/0,,20038039,00.html.

# Bibliography

**BOOKS**

Kawakami, Tim. *Golden Boy: The Fame, Money and Mystery of Oscar De La Hoya.* Kansas City: Andrews McMeel Publishing, 1999.

**WEB SITES**

"Beyond the Glory: Oscar De La Hoya." FoxSports.com. Available online. *http://msn.foxsports.com/other/story/976614.*

Brady, James. "In Step with Oscar De La Hoya." Parade. Available online. *http://www.parade.com/articles/editions/2007/edition_04-22-2007/In_Step_With...Oscar_de_la_Hoya.*

"De La Hoya, Battling Businessman." Business Week. Available online. *http://www.businessweek.com/magazine/content/05_32/b3946102.htm.*

"De La Hoya: What Next?" Sportstar Weekly! Available online. *http://www.hinduonnet.com/tss/tss3029/stories/20070721503402400.htm.*

"Genaro Hernadez." Wikipedia. Available online. *http://en.wikipedia.org/wiki/Genaro_Hernandez.*

Graham, Tim. "De La Hoya Should Have His Way vs. Vargas." ESPN Boxing. Available online. *http://espn.go.com/boxing/columns/graham_tim/1429503.html.*

Gregg, John. "Too Much Oscar for Castillejo." The Boxing Times. Available online. *http://www.boxingtimes.com/analyses/2001/010623delahoya_castillejo.html.*

Gregg, John. "De La Hoya Gets Very Lucky With Sturm." The Boxing Times. Available online. *http://www.boxingtimes.com/analyses/2004/040605delahoya_sturm.html.*

Hammel, Sara. "Oscar De La Hoya to Be a Father—Again." People Magazine Online. Available online. *http://www.people.com/people/article/0,,20038039,00.html.*

Iole, Kevin. "Mosley Makes His Mark: Underdog Wins in Split Decision Over De La Hoya." Las Vegas-Review Journal. Available online. *http://www.reviewjournal.com/lvrj_home/2000/Jun-18-Sun-2000/sports/13798263.html.*

Iole, Kevin. "Oscar's Legacy." Yahoo Sports! Available online. *http://sports.yahoo.com/box/news?slug=kioscar050507&prov=yhoo&type=lgns.*

Iole, Kevin. "Loss Spurs Talk About Retirement." Las Vegas-Review Journal. Available online. *http://www.reviewjournal.com/lvrj_home/2000/Jun-18-Sun-2000/sports/13801442.html.*

"Lamar Williams." BoxRec. Available online. *http://www.boxrec.com/ boxer_display.php?boxer_id=049213.*

"New Cancer Center Provides Important Services to the Community." White Memorial Hospital Press Release. Available online. *http:// www.whitememorial.com/content/news/2000/040500_cancer.asp.*

Ortiz, Nelson. "Oscar De La Hoya Marries Singer Millie Corretjer in Puerto Rico." Latino Sports Legends. Available online. *http://www. latinosportslegends.com/2001/Delahoya_weds_Millie_Corretjer_in_ P.R.-100701.htm.*

"Oscar De La Hoya." Hispanic Heritage. Gale Resources. Available online. *http://www.gale.com/free_resources/chh/bio/delahoya_o.htm.*

"Oscar De La Hoya." Business Week Magazine. Available online. *http:// www.businessweek.com/magazine/content/05_32/b3946102.htm.*

"Oscar De La Hoya." Wikipedia. Available online. *http://en.wikipedia. org/wiki/Oscar_de_la_Hoya.*

"Oscar De La Hoya." Latino Sports Legends. Available online. *http://www.latinosportslegends.com/Delahoya_Oscar_bio.htm.*

"Oscar De La Hoya Steps into New Ring." Cnn.com. Available online. *http://transcripts.cnn.com/TRANSCRIPTS/0012/16/smn.09.html.*

"Oscar De La Hoya." Answers.com. Available online. http://www. answers.com/topic/oscar-de-la-hoya?cat=entertainment.

Perez, Javier. "Oscar De La Hoya vs. Felix Trinidad: A Fight Frozen In Time." East Side Boxing. Available online. *http://www.eastsidebox- ing.com/news.php?p=7543&more=1.*

Sugar, Bert. "De La Hoya-Vargas Post-Fight Analysis." HBO Boxing. Available online. *http://www.hbo.com/boxing/events/2002/0914_ delahoya_vargas/columns/index.html.*

U.S. Census Quick Facts. Available online. *http://quickfacts.census.gov/ qfd/states/06/06037.html.*

Winton, Richard. "L.A. Home Turf for Hundreds of Neighborhood Criminal Groups." Time.com. Available online. http://www.lacp. org/2005-Articles-Main/LAGangsInNeighborhoods.html.

# Further Reading

Saraceno, Jon. *12 Rounds With Oscar De La Hoya: An Illustrated Tribute to Boxing's Brightest Star*. New York: Beckett Publishers, 1998.

Torres, John Albert. *Sports Great Oscar De La Hoya*. Berkeley Heights, NJ: Enslow Publishers, 1999.

## WEB SITES

American Family, Journey of Dreams: East LA: Past and Present. PBS
*http://www.pbs.org/americanfamily/eastla.html*

County of Los Angeles Public Library: East L.A: Community History
*http://www.colapublib.org/history/eastla/*

Golden Boy Promotions
*http://www.goldenboypromotions.com/*

MSN Encarta Encyclopedia: Boxing
*http://encarta.msn.com/encyclopedia_761571782_1/Boxing.html*

# Picture Credits

# Index

# About the Authors

**Susan Muaddi Darraj** is associate professor of English at Harford Community College in Bel Air, Maryland. She is also the author of *The Inheritance of Exile*, published by University of Notre Dame Press.

**Rob Maaddi** is the Philadelphia sports editor/writer for The Associated Press. He is also the host of "The Rob Maaddi Show" weekly on ESPN 920 radio in Philadelphia.